HEALING AFTER LOSS

Also by Martha Whitmore Hickman

For Adults

HOW TO MARRY A MINISTER
THE GROWING SEASON: THE SIGHTS AND SOUNDS OF MIDDLE LIFE
I WILL NOT LEAVE YOU DESOLATE: SOME THOUGHTS FOR
   GRIEVING PARENTS
WAITING AND LOVING: THOUGHTS OCCASIONED BY THE
   ILLNESS AND DEATH OF A PARENT
FULLNESS OF TIME: SHORT STORIES OF WOMEN AND AGING
SUCH GOOD PEOPLE
A DAY OF REST: CREATING SPIRITUAL SPACE IN YOUR WEEK
WADE IN THE WATER: 52 REFLECTIONS ON THE FAITH WE SING

For Children

I'M MOVING
MY FRIEND WILLIAM MOVED AWAY
THE REASON I'M NOT QUITE FINISHED TYING MY SHOES
EEPS, CREEPS, IT'S MY ROOM!
LAST WEEK MY BROTHER ANTHONY DIED
WHEN JAMES ALLEN WHITAKER'S GRANDFATHER CAME TO STAY
GOOD MANNERS FOR GIRLS AND BOYS
WHEN OUR CHURCH BUILDING BURNED DOWN
LOST AND FOUND
WHEN ANDY'S FATHER WENT TO PRISON
AND GOD CREATED SQUASH: HOW THE WORLD BEGAN
ROBERT LIVES WITH HIS GRANDPARENTS
A BABY BORN IN BETHLEHEM
THEN I THINK OF GOD

HEALING AFTER LOSS

Daily Meditations for Working Through Grief

MARTHA WHITMORE HICKMAN

WILLIAM MORROW

An Imprint of HarperCollins*Publishers*

NEW YORK · LONDON · TORONTO · SYDNEY

HarperCollins books may be purchased for educational, business, or sales promotional use. For information please write: Special Markets Department, HarperCollins Publishers Inc., 195 Broadway, New York, NY 10007.

First Avon edition published 1994.

Reprinted in Perennial 2002.

Library of Congress Cataloging-in-Publication Data:
Hickman, Martha Whitmore.
    Healing after loss : daily meditations for working through grief / Martha Whitmore Hickman.
        p. cm.
    1. Grief—Religious aspects—Christianity—Meditations.
2. Consolation—Meditations. 3. Bereavement—Religious aspects—Christianity—Meditations. 4. Devotional calendars. I. Title.
BV4905.2H52   1994   94-11937
242'.4—dc 20   CIP

ISBN 0-380-77338-4

                    20 21 22 LSC 70

Permissions

To Bill and Sudie

Introduction

After the loss of a loved one there is, at first, a great buzz of activity as we make arrangements, as family and friends come together. There is comfort in the close press of friends, in shared tears and hugs, in gifts of food, in re-membering. Religious services give meaning and hope as the community gathers around us in love and support.

But then the services are over, relatives and friends go home, and we are left to enter a new and strange land—a land where one of the persons who has given meaning to our life is gone.

Now there are spaces in the mind, spaces in the days and nights. Often, when we least expect it, the pain and the preoccupation come back, and back—sometimes like the rolling crash of an ocean wave, sometimes like the slow ooze after a piece of driftwood is lifted and water and sand rise to claim their own once more.

This process goes on for a very long time. For years, not for days or months, if the loved one has been close. Some losses—a child, a spouse—are never "got over." But if we are wise and fortunate and have the courage and support to tread the hallowed ground again and again, the loss will begin to lose its controlling power. We will be able to choose. We will be able to walk back from a danger zone if we need to, or save it for a time when we feel stronger. We will be able to feel the spray on our face without a fear of drowning, even to savor the taste of the salt on our lips because, in addition to the poignancy of loss come the rush of love for the one we have lost and perhaps a sense that in the mystery of the universe, we still inhabit that universe together and are tied together in a love that cannot come untied.

"What is essential does not die but clarifies," wrote Thornton Wilder. And again, "The greatest tribute to the dead is not grief but gratitude." Eventually, we will find our way through this particular "valley of the shadow," and while there may always be a tinge of sadness, there will come a sense of our own inner strength and our ability to rejoice in the life we have shared, and to look toward a future in which the loved one, though not physically present, continues to bless us.

Each of us speaks and writes out of our own history of sorrow and gladness. My life as a writer and as a human being has been heavily affected by my experience with grieving—in particular, by the death of a sixteen-year-old daughter who, on a bright summer afternoon while our family was on vacation in the Colorado mountains, fell from a horse and died. It was a long time ago. Grief takes its time, and for a while it occupies all our time. I know whereof I speak.

So it was with a particular sense of being in the right place, of congruence with my own life, that I undertook this book of meditations for those who grieve. The meditations follow the course of the year, but you can start anywhere—in any month, on any day. They are brief because, particularly in the early stages of grieving, our attention span is short, and a seminal thought will serve us better than an extended discussion.

I am grateful to many people for making this book possible—to the family and friends who upheld me when I was most vulnerable; to the spiritual and religious communities who love me and remind me of who I am, who I have chosen to be.

And in particular, now, my thanks to my editor, Lisa Considine, who first approached me about taking on this project; and to the hundreds of people whose words—in chance conversation, in letters, or through the printed page—form the flash points for these meditations. To acquaint, or reacquaint, myself with these sages has been a rich adventure for me. And I hope that, together, we will be able to help those who grieve to move with resoluteness and courage and with trust in a gathering light on the long road to recovery and reclamation of life.

Nashville, Tennessee
August, 1994

HEALING
AFTER LOSS

> . . . I put down these memorandums of my affections
> In honor of tenderness,
> In honor of all of those who have been
> Conscripted into the brotherhood
> Of loss . . .
>
> —EDWARD HIRSCH

When we are drawn into the brotherhood or sisterhood of loss, tenderness seems to be our natural state. We are so vulnerable. Everything brushes against the raw wound of our grief, reminding us of what we have lost, triggering memories—a tilt of the head, a laugh, a way of walking, a touch, a particular conversation. These images are like beads strung together on the necklace of loss. Tenderly, we turn them again and again. We cannot bear them. We cannot let them go.

Then, gradually, bit by bit, the binding thread of grief somehow transmutes, reconstitutes itself as a thread of treasured memories—a tilt of the head, a laugh, a way of walking, a touch, a particular conversation as gifts from the life we shared with the one we have lost, gifts that can never be taken away.

May I honor—and trust—the processes of grief and of healing, knowing that, in time, a new day will come.

January 2

The mind has a dumb sense of vast loss—that is all. It will take mind and memory months and possibly years to gather the details and thus learn and know the whole extent of the loss.

—Mark Twain

In case we are feeling driven to somehow "get done with" our grieving (if I do it faster, maybe I will feel better sooner), let us be reminded that, as in many of life's profoundest experiences—making love, eating, and drinking—faster is not necessarily better. Perhaps the reassuring thing about grieving is that the process will not be cheated. It will take as much time as it needs. Our task is to be attentive when the messages of mind and memory come. If we let them go by unattended the first time, they will probably cost more in the long run.

If I can let my resistance down, be calm in my soul, my grief will tell me what it needs from me at each step along the way.

Love the moment, and the energy of that moment will spread beyond all boundaries.

—Corita Kent

One of the most healing things it is possible to do when one is experiencing profound grief is to try to isolate occasional wonderful moments from the stream of time.

While we may wonder—*How can I bear it, all those years ahead without him/her?*—we live our lives in moments, hours, days. The future *will* have its aspect of emptiness. But if this moment is wonderful—this gathering of dear ones, this walk in the woods, this exchange with a child, this bite of apple, this cup of tea—let's savor it.

I once participated in a human relations workshop on setting limits—a task at which I, like many women, am often neither wise nor skilled. The exercise was to walk around in the roomful of people, imagining you were enclosed in a transparent globe, the dimensions of which were of your own choosing. It was a wonderfully freeing adventure—this imagined moment of being-without-connection. Perhaps in just such a way we can try to cherish the good moments of our lives. Instead of thinking: *Before this I was sad. After this I will be sad*, we could try: *For now, I will be in this moment only and relish its goodness.*

Sometimes the long view is not what I need. I need this moment, without hostage to past or future, experienced for itself alone.

January 4

It is the nature of grace always to fill spaces that have been empty.

—Goethe

Not that we can't tell the difference. Not that we are being disloyal. But if life gives us something else to do with all those impulses toward the one no longer with us, how can we not be grateful? It's like an extra inheritance—a blessing, even—from the one we have lost, going to someone else who needs what we have to give. So we are refreshed by the memory of the loved one, and at the same time offering a gift, creating a new relationship.

Keep me on the lookout for someone who needs me now.

When we need these healing times, there is nothing better than a good long walk. It is amazing how the rhythmic movements of the feet and legs are so intimately attached to cobweb cleaners in the brain.

—ANNE WILSON SCHAEF

Sometimes it's the last thing in the world we feel like doing—getting out and being physically active. Aside from the effort it takes to get up and move, who cares whether we keep our body in good working order anyway?

This is one of the times when thinking has to overcome feeling. We know exercise is "good for us." It's hard to continue to feel depressed when muscles are working vigorously, when we are paying attention to covering ground or swimming through water. As we release physical energy in these rhythmic motions, part of the energy of grief rides away, too. Part of the psychic value of such activity, I suspect, is that we are witnessing our own competence, our ability to move rhythmically, to be "in charge" of our bodies. Our sense of self-confidence will spread. Maybe we won't be forever captive to grief after all. The physical invigoration of exercise invigorates our spirits as well.

Sometimes when I am feeling down, I am my own worst enemy. Let me be my friend.

January 6

The best way to know God is to love many things.
—Vincent van Gogh

After a severe loss, it is hard to venture any new love, let alone to nourish wisely the loves that we have. We are consumed by our loss. What do we have to give? And if we venture a new love, what is to protect us from the same thing happening again?

Nothing. Yet the wisdom of the ages is that the way to find life is to pour our love out on the rest of creation.

I remember, as a child in the aftermath of my first experience with death, thinking that the best way to shield myself from devastation at the other losses which were bound to occur in life was to love as many people as possible. Then when one of them died, I'd still have all those others left to love. I don't know that the geometry of love works quite that way, but it wasn't bad for starters!

To be vulnerable is to be human at the most profound and enriching level.

> Regret is an appalling waste of energy. You can't build
> on it. It is only for wallowing in.
>
> —KATHERINE MANSFIELD

Of course there are things we regret. Things we wish we'd
done differently. Even where there has been time to say
all the appropriate things, images will flash in our minds
that we'd give a lot to be able to change. Surely our loved
one has forgiven us. Can we forgive ourselves?

*I'm sorry. Please know that I loved you. I know that you loved
me.*

JANUARY 8

Hope is the thing with feathers
That perches in the soul
And sings the tune without the words
And never stops at all.

—EMILY DICKINSON

Sometimes we know hope as much by its absence as by its presence. When we're depressed, hope seems almost unknowable, a total illusion. We feel inwardly flattened, unable to move, or as if we are just going through the motions. The song of hope of which the poet speaks is muted. Yet the will of the spirit, as well as of the body, is for life, even for zestful life. Then something happens—a friend calls and we mobilize ourselves, making an effort to be useful, to ourselves or to someone else. The energy quickens. At least the moment has some meaning again and that persistent note of hope, without which we cannot live, starts thrumming in our minds once more.

Sometimes all I can hope for is that I'll feel more hopeful tomorrow.

Something quite unexpected has happened. It came this morning early. For various reasons, not in themselves at all mysterious, my heart was lighter than it had been for many weeks. . . . And suddenly, at the very moment when, so far, I mourned H. least, I remembered her best. Indeed it was something (almost) better than memory; an instantaneous, unanswerable impression. To say it was like a meeting would be going too far. Yet there was that in it which tempts one to use those words. It was as though the lifting of the sorrow removed a barrier.

—C. S. LEWIS

Sometimes we are unconsciously fearful that if we begin to move away from our grief, we will lose what contact we have with the one we miss so much. But maybe it is like letting go of one's children when they are ready to move off on their own. If we loosen our grip, the chances of their returning are much greater, and in ways that are commensurate with who they are now. Perhaps the relinquishing of our most intense grief makes a space into which a new relationship with the loved one can move. It is the *person*, after all, whom we want, not the grief.

May I hold my grief lightly in my hand so it can lift away from me. My connection to the one I have lost is inviolate; it cannot be broken.

JANUARY 10

The earth is my sister. I love her daily grace, her silent daring, and how loved I am. How we admire the strength in each other, all that we have lost, all that we have suffered, all that we know. We are stunned by this beauty, and I do not forget, what she is to me, what I am to her.

—SUSAN GRIFFITH

The earth will help us. There is such strength in the ground, the trees, the water. The air we breathe washes over us with new life. Water is drawn into the atmosphere and returns to fill rivers and streams. The mountains rise up, are worn away, and rise again. On the high tundra tiny flowers bloom unseen. The cycle of the seasons is alive with the promise of rebirth. Creation is a mystery, and so is death. But there are clues, and promises. We are children of God.

In life, as in death, we draw our power from the same source.

You could put the meaning of original sin this way: given a choice we would rather sulk than rejoin the party.
—ROBERT FARRAR CAPON

Often with loss, especially if it has been sudden and untimely, we are tempted to dig in our heels at the last moment before the loss occurred. We will resist. We do not consent.

It is a way of trying to hold on to the loved one, the person we knew before tragedy struck. It is also a form of denial. To rejoin life is to accept what has happened. But it is unacceptable. We will hold our breath, living in a suspended state of noncompliance, until the universe relents, changes its mind—or at least apologizes, acknowledging its crime.

This will not happen. It is we who will be bypassed. Better, as soon as possible, to realize that the terms are different now, and begin to live in this changed reality.

Anger is okay. Denial will hurt no one but me and those I love.

JANUARY 12

In the months after my daughter's death, I filled four notebooks with entries—writing sometimes daily, sometimes several times a day, sometimes only once in several days. I described feelings, the events of the day, occasions of recall, of sorrow and hope. It was a means of moving the grief away, getting it down somewhere else, siphoning it off.

—MARTHA WHITMORE HICKMAN

It may not be writing that is helpful to you. Perhaps talking with friends will have a similar effect. Or painting, or sculpture. The artist Käthe Kollwitz made a whole series of drawings in the aftermath of the death of her son.

The important thing for most of us is not that we have made something of artistic value, but that we have taken a grief that lies like a lump against our hearts, and moved it away from us.

The value of having some pages on which we have recorded our feelings—as opposed to talking with friends—is that we can go back to the pages if we want to. We may never want to, but it relieves us of the pressure of having so much unresolved turmoil in our heads. Try putting it on paper. It may help you sort things out, and you will be free to move on into the next moments of your life.

I will be open to new ways of resolving my grief.

I think these difficult times have helped me to understand better than before how infinitely rich and beautiful life is in every way and that so many things that one goes around worrying about are of no importance whatsoever.

—Isak Dinesen

It is a costly wisdom, and God knows we would not have asked for it. But it is also true that coming through a great sorrow can make us stronger, teach us what is really important.

But to survive the death of a loved one is no guarantee of greater wisdom. We can also become embittered, reclusive, grasping. That's when we need friends, communities of faith, even professional help. But if we can weather the storm, we will have a better sense of who we are and what we want most in life. And we will learn to savor and cherish cool water, sunshine and wind, the smell of roses—and the love and friendship we have now.

I will take time to notice the gifts life gives me, and be thankful.

January 14

Weeping is perhaps the most human and universal of all relief measures.

—Dr. Karl Menninger

Guess what? What women have known for a long time and maybe men are beginning to discover—crying really does make you feel better. And for good reason. Now we are learning that crying has helpful physiological as well as psychological effects.

Researchers at the University of Minnesota have found that emotional tears (as opposed to those shed from exposure to wind, say, or a cut onion) contain two important chemicals, leucine-enkephalin and prolactin, and that the first of these is thought to be related to one of the body's natural pain-relieving substances. Tears are, they tell us, an exocrine substance—like sweat, or exhaled air—and one of the functions of such processes is to help cleanse the body of substances that accumulate under stress.

Then why are we embarrassed by our tears? Why are we fearful they will make others uncomfortable? Often, when people can cry, the work of healing can begin.

No more apologies. No more uneasiness. My tears are for my healing. Perhaps, too, my tears will give others permission to cry when they feel the need.

Keep the door to her life open.

—EDITH FOGG HICKMAN

How many of us know people who, out of grief, hardly ever mention again the name of a loved one who has died? As though the mere speaking the name will bring the rush of grief back in unendurable strength. And as though to avoid the name is somehow to avoid the grief.

This device doesn't work.

When my daughter died, her great-grandmother, who had also endured the loss of an adolescent child, wrote to us, "Keep the door to her life open." I think we would have done it anyway—spoken of her, with decreasing heaviness as the time passed, but it helped to have this dear woman's wisdom right then.

Though the loved one has died, the memory, the sense of the person's presence, has not—nor the possibility, after a while, of taking continuing joy not only in the reminiscences from the past, but in the extension of the person's spirit into our ongoing lives.

Into the nebulous, ongoing mystery of life I welcome, as if through an open door, the continuing spirit of the one I have loved.

JANUARY 16

Whoever survives a test, whatever it may be, must tell the story. That is his duty.

—ELIE WIESEL

Surviving the loss of a loved one is its own kind of test. What does it mean, that it's our duty to tell our story?

To tell our story is a way of affirming the life of the one we have lost—the experiences we had together, the favorite family stories. To tell the story is also a way of moving our grief along, and so contributes to our own healing.

But it is also a gift to others—to tell not only the shared story of the life that has passed, but our own story in relation to this event—how we got through it. What were our fears, our panics? What helped us? What saved the day? If there was a moment when we felt light break through, what was that like?

Our friends will come to their crises of loss soon enough. Perhaps we can ease the way for them. See—it's all right to cry. It's all right to rely on other people. It's all right to be confused and not know what to do. And if there are moments of light and hope, of wonderful support and faith—why, we need to tell those stories, too.

In the telling of my story, I share what is most precious to me.

We are real friends now because we have been able to
share some painful experiences in our private lives.
—MAY SARTON

How quickly friendships are formed when grief is shared.
Visiting my mother in the hospital soon after my daughter's death, I fell into conversation with one of the nurses
on the floor. I don't know which of us got to it first, she
or I. But we were both mothers grieving for an adolescent
child who had recently died. The usual slow, guarded,
back-and-forth dance of getting to know someone went
out the window. We knew each other. We knew the pain,
the questions, in each other's hearts.

I left the city—and my new friend. We exchanged
Christmas messages for a number of years. And though
we live a thousand miles apart, were we to see each other
tomorrow, we would rise to that friendship as though we
had been together just yesterday.

Sometimes it is hard for people we know who haven't
had an experience like ours to know how to relate to us.
We can help them by talking about who we are now, in
this new aspect of our lives. But how blessed we are to
find friends who know, right away, what we are feeling.

*With you, dear companion in sorrow, I can find comfort, and
rest.*

JANUARY 18

Dying is a wild night and a new road.
—EMILY DICKINSON

One of the things so astonishing and costly about losing a loved one is that, while the sun continues to rise and set, newspapers continue to be delivered, traffic lights still change from red to green and back again, our whole life is turned around, turned upside down.

Is it any wonder we feel disoriented, confused? Yet the people we pass on the street are going about their business as though no one's world has been shaken to the core, as though the earth has not opened and swallowed us up, dropped us into a world of insecurity and change.

It is, as Emily Dickinson says, "a new road"—for us as surely as for the one we have lost. It will take us time to learn to walk that road. Time, and a lot of help, so we don't stumble and fall irretrievably. Those who have had their own experiences of loss will probably be our most helpful guides—knowing when to say the right word, when to be silent and walk beside us, when to reach out and take our hand. In time, we will be helpers for others.

I have entered a new country. I will be patient with myself. I will look for companions of the way.

Trade with the gifts God has given you.

—HILDA OF WHITBY

At no time more than when we are grieving do we need to pay attention to the person we are. Something vastly important has been taken away. What are we left with? What else that is important to us is still here?

A grieving man asks a spiritual guide, "What can I do to regain my equilibrium?"

The guide says, "You are tired. Sit in a lounge chair in the sun and get in touch with how your body feels. Listen to what your breathing tells you. Feel the muscles in your legs. Then let your mind wander. Listen to your thoughts. What rises to the top? What calls to you?"

An inner conversation like this may help those of us who are grieving "get back on track" once more. Are there hobbies we value and haven't paid much attention to? Projects we have waited until "later" to pursue? Some work of service we had enjoyed but seem to have moved away from? To pick up some of the important threads we may have set aside is to hasten the reweaving of our life into a coherent pattern again.

I will be on the lookout today for ways to use the unique gifts God has given me.

January 20

Pain is the most individualizing thing on earth. It is true that it is the great common bond as well, but that realization comes only when it is over. To suffer is to be alone. To watch another suffer is to know the barrier that shuts each of us away by himself. Only individuals can suffer.
—EDITH HAMILTON

It is all very well to talk about the universality of grief. But at the time of our loss we feel as though we are the only person in the world who has the feelings we have—and we are right. If well-meaning friends say to us, "I know just how you feel," we inwardly bristle with denial—*No, no. You couldn't know what this is like.*

Even our closest family members have a different experience than we, and sometimes we stumble all over one another, hurt one another, and feel hurt ourselves because we assume that since we are grieving for the same person, our grief is the same.

And yet . . . and yet . . . At no time do we need other people more. There is a fine balance called for between our need to honor the sanctity of our own inner space and our need for others to be present—for love, for company, for understanding support.

I would say to my friends—When I cannot come out from my house of grief, put your hand to the open window and I will hold on for dear life.

Blessed are those who mourn, for they will be comforted.
—MATTHEW 5:4

In the catalog of only nine teachings Jesus gave his disciples on how best to live one's life, this comes second. Mourning is integral to life, it is a part of everyone's life, and its outcome is certain. To mourn is to be comforted.

But how quickly we would turn away from it if we could. Mourning itself is anything but comfortable.

That's not what is promised in Jesus' teaching.

What is promised is that those with the courage to mourn will find, in the wake of mourning, a strange blessing: that after the sadness is expressed, the pain released into the accepting air, it is as though some love at the heart of life wraps its arms around the mourner and says, *There, there, I am with you, I hear you, I understand. Everything's going to be all right.*

In this darkness I will reach out my hand, trusting that life reaches toward me, bringing me comfort and strength to prevail.

JANUARY 22

Part of the process [of rebirth] is the growth of a new relationship with the dead . . . that *veritable ami mort* Saint-Exupéry speaks of. Like all gestation, it is a slow, dark, wordless process. While it is taking place one is painfully vulnerable. One must guard and protect the new life growing within—like a child.

—ANNE MORROW LINDBERGH

It is over shaky ground—this journey between the relationship we had when the person was alive and the relationship we come to have with the dead. We don't know what to expect, don't even know what we're looking for. Are we fooling ourselves, conjuring up the possibility that we can have a relationship with someone who's died?

Perhaps it is a little like a first-time parent who, anxious that something may go wrong, has to keep going back and checking on the baby. Is the baby all right? Still breathing? Still peacefully sleeping?

After a while the parent becomes more confident. The baby really *is* there, and safe, but as with other miracles, this miracle of birth takes getting used to. Perhaps in like manner comes the slowly dawning confidence that in the mystery of living, it is possible to have an ongoing relationship with the dead.

I will open my heart in trust that, in ways I do not now understand, my loved one will continue to be present in my life.

Life only demands from you the strength you possess.
Only one feat is possible—not to have run away.
—DAG HAMMARSKJÖLD

Sometimes we berate ourselves: Why are we not doing better? Particularly if we are people with any pretense to faith, why can we not muster the resources of faith and be a model of calm acceptance and inner serenity?

Because we are human beings and we are hurting.

No one worth his or her salt is going to think less of us if we acknowledge the shattering pain this loss has brought. People may conceivably hold us in some kind of awe if we exhibit an unnatural calm, but they will feel closer to us (and better able to deal with their own grief when their time comes) if they sense we are being honest. We need to let the grief flow through us even as we try to be aware of the ongoing life around us.

Sometimes it is a matter of precisely that—letting the grief flow through us. It is not only, as Hammarskjöld says, the only possible thing to do, it is an act of the utmost courage.

I will not further burden myself by trying to fit some image of a "model griever." The strength I have is the strength to be myself.

JANUARY 24

That day is lost on which one has not laughed.
—FRENCH PROVERB

Even now—maybe especially now—we need humor in our lives. A little comic relief can relieve the tension, save the day.

I remember sitting with my sisters and brother in a small waiting room as my father slept away closer to death, and my brother regaled us with a comic conversation he had overheard. He not only lightened the moment, but acknowledged the strength of the bond among us that, in this extremity, we could trust one another enough to laugh.

I remember a cake brought to our family in the aftermath of a death—a cake so dense that it was characterized by our scientist son as a "neutron star cake." It was eaten with affection and gratitude—a gratitude not only for the cake, but also for the moment of relief and levity it provided.

I remember a small nephew giving an unwittingly hilarious imitation of a bereaved uncle, groaning as he wobbled to his feet.

Disrespectful? Unkind? No. They were blessed moments of saving laughter in a grief-laden day.

Hurray for laughter. Lead me to it!

Time is a dressmaker specializing in alterations.
—Faith Baldwin

Change is the order of life, yet how we resist it.

Sometimes, looking back, we see that only by letting go were we able to move on to new adventures, new insights and satisfactions.

A widow who had lived in her husband's shadow, doing the dutiful wife-and-mother things, emerged after his death as a featured speaker at many church and civic gatherings. She said to me once, "Isn't it a shame I had to wait until he died before I began to come into my own?"

We live our lives in chapters. What was right for her in the early years of her marriage was obviously not suitable in her later years. Nor would she have wanted to consign home and children to someone else's care when her children were small.

There is some consolation in knowing that change, even difficult change, brings surprising gifts. Though the thought may be unappealing to us now, let's not shut the door too soon on something good that could be waiting for us in the next room.

◆◆

I will keep my eyes open. Something surprising and good may happen tomorrow—or the day after.

January 26

Help thy brother's boat across, and lo! thine own has reached the shore.

—Hindu Proverb

One reason self-help and recovery groups are so effective is that they enlist us in helping one another—so that in each transaction two people are helped and our coping muscles are strengthened in helping another through the familiar rapids.

To help another is to forget, for a few moments at least, one's own primary consuming need. We gain a little perspective in knowing we're not the only one.

And, having a similar need, we understand one another, are bonded together in ways that only those who have traveled the same pathway can be. We don't need to explain ourselves. The other knows. He or she has been there.

Initially, in these pairings we will be the needier. Someone who has been there can be our guide, our hope-inducing model.

Then, after a while, we will take our turn as the guide. But even then, the sorrow that lingers will lessen as we bring life-giving hope to another: *See, I made it through. So can you.*

I am grateful for those who reach out to me, and for the opportunities I will have to reach out to others.

And can it be that in a world so full and busy, the loss of one weak creature makes a void in any heart, so wide and deep that nothing but the width and depth of eternity can fill it up!

—CHARLES DICKENS

How could it be? We have many friends, many associations. A good deal of our time we didn't spend exclusively with this loved person who is now gone.

But now! The whole of creation seems to shout out the absence of that one. Even places where we used to be glad to get away to, to be alone—a solitary shopping trip, for instance, or a walk in the park—now speak of absence and loneliness. We see people walking jovially together and think, Why not me?

There is no way we can leave our grief at home when we embark on such ventures. But we can at least avoid compounding the grief by missing something that never was!

I used to be contented often to be alone—sometimes to prefer it. Let me not fall so under the spell of grief that my imagination has no room for being alone and contented now.

JANUARY 28

Feeling better . . . I also felt a sense of betrayal of my husband, even though I rationally knew that sustained grief could be morbid. Because grief may become a substitute for the dead one, giving up our grief can be the greatest challenge of mourning.

—MARY JANE MOFFAT

This may be puzzling to us at first. Surely we know the difference between our grieving and the one for whom we grieve.

But it is easier than we know to confuse the two. The one we love is gone—there is no retrieving that person by thinking about him or her all the time.

But grieving? That is our whole agenda for a while. To that we can give endless attention. We look for the one we have lost by looking through the film of our ever-present grief. We get used to it and it is hard to move away. But we must; otherwise we will be stuck there at our loved one's death, unable to relish the life that person lived.

Many years after the death of her father, a young woman said, "Finally, I am able to remember my father's life, not just his death."

I look forward to the day when images of my loved one's life are no longer associated with the event of my loved one's death.

Even desolation is a world to be explored.
                              —SYLVIA TOWNSEND WARNER

It is a world we do not want to enter, a world for which we have no hunger. We would turn from it if we could. Yet we find ourselves in it. And our company is a multitude.

There is a story of a woman who came to the Buddha seeking help after the death of her child and was told that, for healing, she need only find a mustard seed from a household that had never known sorrow. According to the story, she traveled over all the world in vain, never finding such a household, but found instead—understanding, compassion, friendship, and truth.

The world of desolation is a world that calls many of us. There is no going around it. There is only going through it, if we are to find healing and new life. It is a world worth exploring and it offers to us those same qualities the bereaved mother found—understanding, compassion, friendship, truth.

◆◆

Nothing is to be gained by turning away from the truth. When the circumstances of my life are grim, I will face the grimness, learn what it has to teach me, and walk on through.

JANUARY 30

Healing is impossible in loneliness; it is the opposite of loneliness. Conviviality is healing. To be healed we must come with all the other creatures to the feast of Creation.
—WENDELL BERRY

These are hard words to hear, because often when we are grieving, our impulse is to withdraw from other people. *There they are, carrying on their ordinary lives when my world has fallen apart. How can they understand? Besides, my sadness will make them uncomfortable, won't it?*

We will need times of solitude, of course, to be with our thoughts, to take the measure of our grief, to rest. But there is little comfort in being alone, and we need to resume our place in the human family, to realize we are not the center of the world, to let ourselves be enfolded in the loving care of friends.

If there are people who are uncomfortable with our sadness, we can move on. Or if we are brave, we can acknowledge the situation: "I realize I'm not a bundle of cheer right now. But I needed to get out and be with people."

Often this will put other people at ease. The situation was awkward mostly because the unspoken thought hung in the air but was not mentioned—like a stranger who comes to a party and is never introduced.

Sometimes it is hard for me to go into groups. But my connections to other people are the flow of life to me.

God is serious about knowing how it is with us.
—Willie S. Teague

In his best-selling book *When Bad Things Happen to Good People*, Rabbi Harold Kushner writes of his sense of God being present to his suffering and that of his family as his young son grew desperately ill and died. That God did not cause that suffering, but in some way shared it, and was present to comfort and sustain.

A friend tells of driving along one day and having a sudden flash of conviction that God cared for *him*—"that God really loved me, David. I rolled down the car window and sang," he says, and smiles, bemused and grateful.

Listening, I am grateful, too. Yes, I think. I have felt that way sometimes.

To whatever extent we feel creation is more than a random happenstance, surely it must be safe to say that God cares for us. If I had created anything of such magnitude, *I* would pay close attention. *I* would want to know how it was doing.

Sometimes in my darkness I can believe I am held in a love which supports all creation. Not always, but sometimes.

FEBRUARY 1

The man who removed mountains began by carrying away small stones.

—CHINESE PROVERB

How do we start picking up the pieces, rebuilding our lives, after we have sustained a grievous loss?

We won't be able, probably, to undertake major new ventures for a while. But a single step will help, will signify to our inner self that our investment is in life, not in endless grief.

A friend tells me that after she began sewing some new clothes for herself, she began to feel better. It was an investment in living.

It was only a beginning, but I remember the moment in the grocery store when I decided to "look cheerful" instead of carrying around the glum face I had worn for weeks. It was a very small thing, but evidently important. Otherwise I wouldn't remember it after almost twenty years.

I will take a small step—just one. In my mind's eye, perhaps I can see my loved one nodding in encouragement—"Yes. Go on. You can. I am with you."

She thought that she had never before had a chance to realize the strength that human beings have, to endure; she loved and revered all those who had ever suffered, even those who had failed to endure.

—JAMES AGEE

It is true that grief extends our sensibilities. We find we have a sudden kinship with those who have suffered losses similar to ours. We may, like the woman in Agee's story who had been recently widowed, find ourselves in awe of the strength in ourselves to simply go on living in the face of such suffering. We realize how much we have been spared, not to have encountered this kind of grief before, and our hearts go out to those who are young and sustain a major grief too soon, before they have had carefree years to treasure.

All of this comes as a kind of astonishment in the first period of grief. Like our plunging into cold water, it takes our breath away. The shock alters all our perceptions. Then we get used to it. Our bodies warm to it and we begin to swim.

In my ability to endure I see a strength I didn't know I had.

FEBRUARY 3

Silence is the strength of our interior life . . . If we fill our
lives with silence, then we will live in hope.
—THOMAS MERTON

There is a delicate balance between socializing and being
quietly alone. Too much socializing can be an attempt to
run away from our difficult truth. Too much solitude can
leave us brooding and withdrawn.

But wait. Not all silence is in solitude. Quaker meetings
for worship are largely experiences of collective silence.
Sometimes we feel closest to others when we are silent
together.

Still, most silence takes place when we are alone, and
we would do well to recognize its value. Over the past
years we have heard of the physical value of meditative
silence—in lowering blood pressure, slowing the heart,
even facilitating some kinds of healing. We know that under many circumstances a few moments of silence can feed
our spirits.

So in our healing from the wounds of grief, a generous
amount of silence will help us rest into the depths of our
own souls, and find peace.

*I will not be afraid to be still. I will savor the refreshments of
silence. Perhaps the spirit of my loved one will join me there.*

I am not mad:—I would to heaven, I were,
For then, 'tis like I should forget myself:
O, if I could, what grief should I forget!
—WILLIAM SHAKESPEARE

Grief has indeed pushed men and women over the edge into insanity. Sometimes we may have felt this way ourselves: If I could only go crazy . . . anything to get away from this terrible consciousness of loss.

Fortunately, such moments pass. If we have been close at all to the lives of the mentally ill, we know this is no reprieve from suffering.

And if at times of extreme stress we have felt as though our own safeguards to reason and reality are blurring, we know that slipping away from reality is no pathway to peace of mind and heart—any more than overindulgence in drugs or alcohol is a valid way to deal with sorrow.

But we understand the impulse, and nod in grateful recognition when we read of others who have had similar feelings.

Knowing I have company in my struggle can help me see my way through.

FEBRUARY 5

As for inflicting our sorrow on other people, one does not want to go around blathering and crying all the time. But perhaps it is our gift to others to trust them enough to share our feelings with them. It may help them deal with some of their own.

—MARTHA WHITMORE HICKMAN

The attempt to "be brave," to "keep a stiff upper lip" and otherwise be controlled and poised in the face of grief, is a false god. How are we *supposed* to feel when our heart is broken?

And yet we continue to extol those who do not show their grief in public, who receive condolences as though the occasion were a pleasant Sunday afternoon exchange. "She was so brave. I was proud of her. She didn't break down, not once," we hear people say.

For whose benefit is this ironclad hold on the emotions? For the griever's sake? For the sake of the consolers, who may be fearful of being swept into the grief, unsure of how they will handle it when their time comes?

A friend said, "If someone cries in front of me, I consider it a gift."

I will not further burden myself with false prohibitions about tears.

But such a tide as moving seems asleep,
Too full for sound and foam,
When that which drew from out the boundless deep
Turns again home.

—ALFRED TENNYSON

These words of Tennyson speak powerfully of the sustaining rhythms of creation. We are familiar with the tides of the ocean, the pull of the moon, the rhythmic rotation of stars and planets. And we, who set some of our most holy festivals—Ramadan, Easter, Passover—by the phases of the moon and the orbiting of the earth around the sun, are also part of the rhythmic flow of life.

Can we not hope, and trust, that the rhythms which sweep through the natural world with such resonance continue to sustain our loved one who has passed, for a time, out of the reach of our senses and our rational knowledge?

And can we not imagine the "home" of which Tennyson speaks as being imbued with more nurture and safety and possibilities for growth than anything even the most fortunate of us have experienced?

In the rhythms that flow through us all, I find hope and promise.

FEBRUARY 7

When it is dark enough, you can see the stars.
—CHARLES BEARD

Often it is easiest to see the stars in the long, cold nights of winters.

People who have come through any kind of life-threatening event—a crash, a tornado, a severe illness—speak of how it has changed their perspective. Likewise, when we suffer through the loss of a loved one, it's easier to see what's important.

Several years after our daughter died, we experienced a burglary. All of our wedding silver was stolen, as well as some antique pieces that had been handed down through many generations.

Of course we were upset. But right away the words came to me: "It's only things." I have no way of knowing whether or not I'd have been this calm had the theft occurred before her death, but I suspect not.

The stars are not only clearer, but more beautiful. Ancient navigators found their way through the seas by looking at the stars. So maybe the experience of loss not only helps clarify what is important to us, but also helps us know where we are and the direction in which we want to go.

In the extremity of darkness I will look up and see the stars.

> Recovery is not a process we can will, but consists of experiencing many small deaths, the passing of significant anniversaries, until our identity is solid and natural in the pronoun "I."
>
> —MARY JANE MOFFAT

Do you remember how it was those first weeks and months after your loved one died? The first time you went to the grocery store? The first time you changed the furnace filter? The first time you went to the movies? Nothing was too insignificant to note. And, of course, the milestones like birthdays and Christmas shouted their warning weeks ahead of time.

And then, perhaps after months, perhaps after years, you feel like a whole person again. The hurt is still there, but it has become part of your inner self. You no longer feel as though part of your own being has been torn away and that everything bumps against that open wound.

I knew a significant change had occurred for me when, upon being asked, "How many children do you have?" I said, "I have three sons," and didn't need to add, "I had a daughter who died." That was still integral to me, but I didn't need to say it every time.

I will trust this process to unfold in its own time.

FEBRUARY 9

Light griefs can speak; great ones are dumb.

—SENECA

We are urged, for our own health, to "talk about it." Sometimes we can, sometimes we can't.

It would be bad news indeed if this inability to speak lasted very long. But, as in many other aspects of the grieving process, our psyches know what we need.

So if in our grief we are at "a loss for words," we don't need to be talking on and on. Certainly we don't need to talk constantly in order to help other people feel more comfortable. It's okay to expect them to adapt to our needs now, instead of the other way around.

I remember going to a party and, in contrast to my usual eagerness to be part of the conversational exchange, feeling in my grief unable to do that. Like a mother giving permission to a child to be excused from some task, I gave myself permission to be a bystander, on the edge of the conversation with no "duty" to grease the social wheels. The group got along fine without me, and I can still remember the inner sigh of relief as I settled into my small psychic cocoon—for a little while.

It's okay for me to take care of myself right now.

> In the midst of winter I discovered that there was in me an invincible summer.
>
> —ALBERT CAMUS

It surprises us. We know it's a fluke. We know it won't last. Happiness? Contentment? Joy?

And not just a quick flash of joy, of contentment—as when we are lifted up on wings of song—or by prayer—or by a spectacular sky—or because of a daisy blooming in some field. But a sense that in some way we are going to be able, after all this, to be happy! Whoever would have thought it?

That assurance, too, may slip away. But it will come back. Perhaps each time it will seem less like an astonishing stranger, someone come to visit us in disguise. No, it is real—this fecundity, this extended daylight, this warmth, this beauty of a summer evening. Even in the wintry distress of our pain, we will believe in summer.

Summer has its storms, too. But they will pass. Maybe they will clear the air, and bring the world fresh and clean to our attention once more. It is life calling to us—*See, you are mine. I have wonders in store for you, believe it or not. And I will wait for you—beneath the snow, if necessary, and beyond the storm.*

In the midst of winter I will entertain the possibility that summer will come.

February 11

The problem with death is absence.
—Roger Rosenblatt

After all our attempts to comfort ourselves and to make sense out of dying, we are left with a huge hole in the fabric of our lives—"I miss you. I miss you. I miss you."

And then what?

The absence begins to feel familiar, the edges of the psychic hole grow less sharp, maybe begin to grow together, so we can walk along without being in perpetual danger of falling into the astonishing abyss of the person's death.

In time, the absence even mutates into another kind of presence. Someone has said that a child who dies is with you in a way a living child cannot be. In some ways that's true. And, yes, it is a comfort. This is the case not only with children, but with parents and other loved ones who have died and who become part of the community we carry with us wherever we are.

Perhaps they become our guardian angels, our link with the other side. But to let them go initially is one of the compromises we are forced to make with life, and our longing for them sometimes makes the prospect of our own death almost all right.

I am, and always will be, a part of all that I have known.

It takes more than will power to stop thinking of someone you have loved and lost. I could see that in the slump of his shoulders and the way his feet were set close together. He had tried, in a burst of energetic resolve. But it would take more than that, to stop. Whatever new beauties he would discover in the world would still, for a long time and maybe for his whole life, not be quite enough to keep his memories away.

—JOSEPHINE HUMPHRIES

At first, we have no choice but to think almost constantly of the one we have lost. An hour does not pass that we are not aware of our loss—remembering the person, recalling episodes and moods of our life together, thinking of what can no longer be.

Then maybe one day we are startled to realize that for several hours, maybe even a full day, our thoughts have been elsewhere. We are beginning to heal.

But we do not need to worry that we will lose the memory of those we love. What we need to remember, we will. And sometimes when "new beauties" come, the memory of the loved one shines even more brightly—as we imagine sharing this new joy with the one we have lost. There is pain in this, but perhaps there is also a refreshed sense of the loved one's being.

The memory of my loved one is a part of my life forever.

FEBRUARY 13

Grief dares us to love once more.

—TERRY TEMPEST WILLIAMS

It would be easy, wouldn't it, to somehow close down the valves of loving so we couldn't be hurt this much again?

No, it wouldn't. It's probable that for a while we will feel a kind of numbness, a recoil against the blow we have suffered. But without the love of friends and family, we'd never make it through this time of grieving.

And love calls to love. We are summoned from our grief by love, and we will be healed by love.

But we will not be healed if we don't participate, if we don't answer the love of others by our love for them.

Yes, it takes courage to risk loving again. It is the courage to be most fully human. It is the courage that affirms the love we shared with the one we have lost.

When the time comes, I will be ready.

For everything there is a season . . . a time to break down, and a time to build up; a time to weep, and a time to laugh; a time to mourn, and a time to dance . . .

—ECCLESIASTES 3:1–4

If there is one thing grievers know, it is how changeable our moods can be. One moment we are relatively calm, in control, keeping our grief at bay. The next moment we are overwhelmed, our equilibrium shattered.

Anything can send us off—a fragrance, the words of a song, an article in the newspaper that reminds us of our loss, the first sign of spring—and our loved one not here to share it. Even minor holidays—like Valentine's Day—can send us reeling.

Other times we are carefree, relishing the moment—the beauty of snow, the warmth of fire, the comfort of hot cocoa, the presence of friends. And we wonder why we are so susceptible to such mood swings. We may even wonder about our sanity—When will my moods be more measured so I am not always in danger of being swept away, of falling through the trapdoor of despair?

Our lives have been shattered by loss. Of course it will take time for the pieces to come together in any coherent pattern.

I will be patient with myself, honoring the seasons of my grieving, trusting I am on my way to being healed.

FEBRUARY 15

> Spirituality is that place where the utterly intimate and the vastly infinite meet.
>
> —RICK FIELDS

Among the occasions in human life where such a meeting might take place, surely the experience of death must be high on the list. At one moment the person is there, breathing, alive, and the next moment the body remains, an empty shell, but the person who laughed and cried, who spoke, who loved, is gone.

Where?

People have told of sensing—even seeing—the spirit of the dead standing close. People who report near-death experiences tell of hovering above their body, watching all the frantic goings-on to resuscitate them. People hundreds of miles away at the time of another's death report experiencing a sudden symptom—a flash of pain, perhaps—which later correlates with the time and cause of death of a loved one.

Perhaps our experience with such mysteries is a clue that we know only a small fraction of the Creator's good intention for us. It doesn't take the pain of separation away. But if we can think of it as temporary separation and not permanent—well, that makes all the difference in the world!

I will try to be open to all avenues of wisdom and hope.

Should his heart break and the grief pour out, it would
flow over the whole earth, it seems, and yet, no one sees
it.

—ANTON CHEKHOV

It is an odd feeling to be walking along a busy street, or
going in and out of stores, with a grief so central and preoccupying it seems to define our existence, and yet people
walk by not noticing at all!

Are we puzzled, and perhaps a little angry, that the
world should continue on its merry way? Somehow we
feel the earth should stop spinning and acknowledge our
grief.

But when we stop and think about it, we don't really
want all the rest of the world to go awry, just to keep us
company. We need whatever security an otherwise well-
ordered world might offer. Just as well, then, that these
passersby don't know the turmoil and sorrow within us
as we brush past. And who knows what they may be carrying in their own hearts?

◆◆

*I don't need everyone else to be sucked into my grief, as long as
I can claim my own space for grieving.*

FEBRUARY 17

All the wonderful things in life are so simple that one is not aware of their wonder until they are beyond touch. Never have I felt the wonder and beauty and joy of life so keenly as now in my grief that Johnny is not here to enjoy them.

—FRANCES GUNTHER

Perhaps anything that reminds us how fragile life is evokes this feeling. How could we have taken life's gifts for granted?

It is a poignant realization that our loved one is deprived of these gifts of which we are so newly aware. We almost feel as though we need to experience the world for two people.

Perhaps we can think of our newly enhanced sense of the beauty of the world as a gift from our lost love. We can also comfort ourselves by remembering how, in accounts of near-death experiences, a constant theme is the astonishment at the beauty and light of the world beyond. Perhaps the beauty of this world is but a foretaste of what is to come.

In my savoring of the wonders of this world, I can sense the presence of my love.

This is the Hour of Lead—
Remembered, if outlived,
As Freezing persons recollect the Snow—
First—Chill—then Stupor—then the letting go—
—EMILY DICKINSON

One can scarcely imagine heavier images than those in this poem by Emily Dickinson. Yet the feeling is familiar to us—a heaviness in our step, in our whole body, a heaviness of mind and heart.

The Chill is accurate, too—a kind of pervasive lethargy. We may find it hard to think. We forget where we put something, what we had planned to do. (It's a good time for making lists.)

But we *do* outlive the Hour of Lead. The will of the body and spirit is for recovery—even for growth, for there is no recovery without growth.

◆◆

Even when I am feeling swallowed in an Hour of Lead, I will try to remember there will be a new time, and a new day.

FEBRUARY 19

With the help of these and other commonplace objects—
with the help of the two big elm trees that shaded the
house from the heat of the sun, and the trumpet vine by
the back door, and the white lilac bush by the dining-
room window, and the comfortable wicker porch furniture
and the porch swing that contributed its *creak . . . creak
. . .* to the sounds of the summer night—I got from one
day to the next.

—WILLIAM MAXWELL

When our world is shattered by grief, sometimes the only
things that get us through are the familiar objects and routines that say in their very being, *Look—you have not lost
everything; some things are the same.* They make no demands
on us, these familiar objects, they are just there. They rep-
resent stability in a world that has suddenly fallen to
chaos. We are grateful to them in an irrational, embracing
way, as though they were dear friends—which, in this crisis, they are.

*In this time of upset and change, I am grateful for the solace of
the familiar.*

FEBRUARY 21

I'm for whatever gets you through the night.
—FRANK SINATRA

We all have our ways of dealing with our pain, and the range of acceptable responses is wide. Reason sometimes doesn't have a lot to do with it. A woman whose beloved husband, a cabinetmaker, died suddenly in the prime of life said she began to accept his death when she told herself that God needed the best cabinetmaker in the world. She would never defend this on the grounds of reason. Who cares? It worked for her, and it did no one any harm.

When our daughter died, a friend whose father had died not long before wrote to us. "My dad will look after Mary," she said. It was wonderfully comforting.

Whatever images come to us in our grief that bring us stability and peace are gifts—as welcome and helpful to survival as the casseroles, the cards, and the flowers. They might not stand up under the scrutiny of reason, but experiences of death and grief call for leaps of intuition and imagination. We have entered a new realm.

Before this mystery I open heart and mind to all leadings of the spirit.

To fashion an inner story of our pain carries us into the heart of it, which is where rebirth inevitably occurs.
—SUE MONK KIDD

How to do this? And why?

Some people keep a journal—a useful tool in any event—but maybe especially now, when our lives are apt to be in emotional turmoil. To write down whatever is preoccupying us—snatches of memory, accounts of daily grief and confusion—not only helps us identify and sort out what is happening, but puts all of that in a safe, recorded place where we can get back to it if we want. To write it down relieves us of the need to carry it around in our head all the time.

Some write down stories from the life of the loved one. A dear friend spent several months following his wife's death writing down the story of their courtship, more than sixty-five years ago. It was not only a beautiful story—and a prospective treasure for close family members—but, as he said, "It helped me keep in touch with her."

The fashioning of the inner story will help make order of the chaos into which grief often plunges us—and may even reward us with treasures!

We are called to live with integrity, to express the truth
as we perceive it, and to trust God's ability to use what
we offer.

—ELIZABETH J. CANHAM

And if what we have to offer, right now, is only our pain?
Well, then, let us offer that. If pain and grief are our deepest reality, then we must acknowledge that reality. If we
try to gloss over it, *perpetually* looking the other way, we
will fool no one, especially ourselves. Like a wound that
is not exposed to air and healing light, this wound will
take longer to heal and will cost us more in the long run.

This doesn't mean that we need to spend every moment
of every day wallowing in grief—though there will be
times when that pretty well describes the way we feel. We
will want, both for our own sake and for the sake of those
around us, to put a cap on our grief for a while and relate
to the world in a more casual way.

When grief is fresh and overwhelming, *that* is the truth
as we perceive it, and to act out of that is not only our
own necessity, but also a witness to those around us that
sadness is honorable and to be trusted. The journey
through grief has a varied landscape but no permanent
detours.

◆◆

*My grief is a heavy enough burden right now. I will not add to
that the burden of trying to camouflage who I am.*

FEBRUARY 23

It may be
   that some little root of the sacred tree still lives
Nourish it then
   that it may leaf and bloom and fill with singing birds.
                                                    —BLACK ELK

What is the glimmer of hope that insists on being present to us in our darkness? Is it the lingering spirit of our loved one saying, *I'm all right, don't worry*? Is it our own intuition that there is more to life—and death—than we can possibly understand, that death is not a stopping place but a gate to pass through?

Or is it the unquenchable nature of life, bubbling up, blossoming, singing even in dark hours?

A friend whose son had died tells me of how, in a woodsy glade, a bird previously unknown to that region perched on a high limb in a shaft of light, and sang. And sang. She said that while she continued to have times of great loneliness, never again did she question her son's continuing love and presence, or that ultimately she would be reunited with him.

May I now see the sacred tree, and hear the sound of singing birds.

People bring us well-meant but miserable consolations when they tell us what time will do to help our grief. We do not want to lose our grief, because our grief is bound up with our love and we could not cease to mourn without being robbed of our affections.

—PHILLIPS BROOKS

Of course time eases our grief, provided we let it follow its course and give it its due. Few of us would want the intensity and desolation of early grief to stay with us forever. That's not what we're afraid of.

But we may be afraid that we'll lose the intensity of love we felt for the one we have lost.

At first these two—the grief and the love—are so wedded to each other that we cannot separate them. We may cling to the grief in desperation so we will be sure not to lose the love.

Perhaps the grief and the love will always be wedded to each other to some degree, like two sides of a coin. But maybe after a while, when we flip the coin, it will almost always be the love that turns up on top.

My loved one is as much a part of my life as the air and food and water that nourish my body. Therefore I shall not fear losing someone who has been, and is, a part of me.

She was easily moved to laughter, a youthful, rather shrill laughter that brought tears to her eyes, and which she would afterwards deplore as inconsistent with the dignity of a mother burdened with the care of four children and financial worries. She would master her paroxysms of mirth, scolding herself severely, "Come, now, come! . . ." and then fall to laughing again till her pince-nez trembled on her nose.

—COLETTE

One of the greatest gifts we can give ourselves (and we'll know we've passed a milestone when we're able to do this) is to remember, with delight and laughter, the funny times we shared with our loved one.

At first we have little heart for laughter. Later, when we do, it may seem disrespectful to the dead. Perhaps we even feel guilty.

But think—which would your loved one rejoice in more—seeing you sad, or seeing you reveling in the memory of wonderful, hilarious times together?

A merry heart doeth good like a medicine. Proverbs 17:22

Again rises from the heart of suffering the ancient cry,
O God, why? O God, how long?
And the cry is met with silence.

—JIM COTTER

Some days we seem to be managing pretty well, confident we can face the future. There are other days—and nights—when we feel utterly abandoned, left in a dark room alone, when the universe seems a vast and unfriendly place. It is hard to remember that we ever felt any other way, or believe we'll ever feel better again. Truly we have entered upon "the dark night of the soul." Does it help to know that over the centuries this despair has been shared by many, that even in this desolation we have the company of saints and pilgrims, a myriad of fellow sufferers? For even as our pain is particular to us alone, even as our loved one was unique in all the world, perhaps we can rest back—just a little—on the knowledge that multitudes in the human family have walked where we walk.

While there are things we can do to be ready for a brighter time—get enough rest, eat properly, read, pray, talk with people—the prevailing wisdom seems to be that such dark nights are simply to be endured, waited out. They will not last forever. And one day—perhaps as a surprise—we will realize the cloud has lifted.

If I am feeling down today, it doesn't mean I will forever.

FEBRUARY 27

A theme may seem to have been put aside, but it keeps returning—the same thing modulated, somewhat changed in form.

—MURIEL RUKEYSER

We find reminders everywhere. Not only the anniversaries—one week, one month, a birthday, one year—but the swing of a stranger's shoulders, the line of a cheekbone, or the tilt of a head. Events we went to together, songs we shared, foods we both liked—or disliked—all trigger our emotions. Our life is strewn with these memory buttons that, when touched, plunge us into sorrow.

We need to give these reminders their due—Yes, I recognize you. Yes, you remind me of my loss. But as we grow stronger we can exercise some choice in the matter and, after an initial tender acknowledgment, put the association with our lost love aside.

A few months after my daughter's death, I saw a young woman wearing a plaid jacket similar to one my daughter had owned. I couldn't take my eyes off her. She even had similar coloring, the same long hair. For a moment I thought of going and speaking to her.

Instead, I closed my eyes and prayed for this young stranger—for her life, whatever it was. I don't know that it did her any good, but it did me, and I went back to my reading.

I will see the shadows of my grief everywhere. And move on.

They seemed to come suddenly upon happiness as if they had surprised a butterfly in the winter woods.

—EDITH WHARTON

It comes to us as a revelation at first—an astonishment—almost an occasion of guilt. We can be happy!

Maybe we thought it would not happen, that our life would be forever colored with pain, that no moment would be free of it.

There is a way in which we are right: no moment is ever free of the life history that has preceded it. And we don't want that. One of the things we sometimes fear—needlessly—is that, having lost the loved one, we will lose the memory of the loved one as well. That will not happen.

But we will lose, or be released from, the overhanging cloud of gloom which for a while may seem our daily portion. Part of that is up to us. We *can* decide not to be happy again. It may take a lot of work—never to be happy again—but we can do it if we want to.

How much better—and how much more a tribute to the one we have lost—to walk out from under our cloud, so that when we come upon a butterfly in the winter woods, we will be able to see it!

Gloom has no value of itself. It's fine to be happy.

MARCH 1

Where? Where has it gone, that light, that spark, that love that looked into mine? What has it to do with that cold clay? It's here, here, here in my heart. She's in me, around me. Nothing in that clay.

—ANZIA YEZIERSKA

The change is astonishing when breath and life depart and the body is left. We look at it—loved, revered—but it is only a shell now. The processes that sustained it have stopped. The blood lies still. The chest does not rise and fall.

But where has the person gone? Interpretations differ according to belief and experience. But surely one of the ways a person lives on is in those of us who gather to mourn the passing and to celebrate the life. It's not simply that we will remember loved ones; they live on through things they taught us and in the way they affected our lives.

So that in the weeks, months, and years that lie ahead, we may find qualities and actions in our own lives which surprise us until we smile and think, "I wonder. Yes, maybe that's a part of _____ living in me."

I will welcome and care for the ways in which my loved one continues to live on in me.

Many promising reconciliations have broken down because, while both parties came prepared to forgive, neither party came prepared to be forgiven.
—Charles Williams

Sometimes it is the last stone to be lifted from the grieving
heart—the inability to accept forgiveness. And we each
have our own catalog of things for which we yearn for
forgiveness. The harsh word quickly spoken, the service
performed begrudgingly—or not at all.

Who is holding out for reprisal? Is the one who has died
scowling and shaking an accusing finger in some nether-
world? More than likely it's we who continue to berate
ourselves: How could you?

"When you forgive yourself, you are forgiven," says
Elisabeth Kübler-Ross, who for many years has written
about and consoled others with the stages of grief.

Imagine a conversation between you and the one for
whom you grieve. Would you want that person to be without flaws? Such a person would bear little resemblance to
the one you love.

No more does that person want perfection of you. You
wouldn't be recognizable, either!

*I will try to let the weight of guilt and regret slip away. I am
not perfect. I am loved. And love makes all kinds of allowances—
and keeps on loving.*

MARCH 3

The bell strikes one. We take no note of time
But from its loss.

—EDWARD YOUNG

Time is always slipping away from us. But the loss of a loved one puts its own strong markers on our sense of time. For a while we divide all our experiences into "Before" and "After." Before the death, after the death. Perhaps before the onset of illness, and after the onset of illness. The coloration of the past shifts—all that has gone before is now sealed with a fixative, the sign of an era ended. The time that spins out ahead into the future is, for a while, an empty space, a projected perpetual reminder of loss.

But then, as we begin to reweave our lives with the strands now available to us, the lines of demarcation soften a bit. We begin to look back, not always with the pain of what we have lost, but with joy and appreciation for that life we have shared. And, in a way that we could never have imagined until we had made this journey of loss and grief, we savor the ways in which our loved one still is, and will continue to be, a presence in our lives.

As I begin to see beyond the pain, I sense how both sadness and joy are part of the tapestry of my life.

An individual doesn't get cancer, a family does.
—TERRY TEMPEST WILLIAMS

In facing loss, sharing grief with others in the family can be wonderfully helpful. As we mourn together, tell our common stories, and go over old possessions and memorabilia, we are able to be present to one another in ways no one outside the family circle can possibly be.

But at other times we may be the last person another family member needs in working his or her way through grief.

Why? Because we all have different histories with the one who has died, and different ways of grieving. One member of the family may feel resentful—or heroic—that he or she has carried more of the burden of a parent's long illness. Another, less close, may feel relegated to some kind of second-class status. More reserved members of the family may find the more expressive members jarring and overwrought. The intensity of death and loss can make otherwise acceptable differences in style seem almost intolerable, and it may help us get through some difficult times if we can accept both the graces and the hazards of sharing our loss with one another.

◆◆

In this loss, as I draw strength from my family, I also acknowledge and honor the fact that we each grieve in our own way.

March 5

Faith
is the bird
that feels the light
And sings
when the dawn
is still dark.

—Rabindranath Tagore

In this season of early spring, midway between winter and summer solstices, sometimes, waking in the morning, we can almost feel the first touches of summer coming. Often it is still cold and dark. But something in the air confirms what the calendar is telling us—that the days, at least in our Northern Hemisphere, are lengthening. The light will come sooner and last longer.

Once, in a time of mourning, I was awake all night long. We had overnight visitors. We had stayed up late talking. It was after midnight when we went to bed, and then I didn't sleep. I was feeling restless, anxious. And then, in the early morning darkness, the birds began to sing.

Already? I thought.

May we, in our season of darkness and sorrow, hear—and sometimes as a surprise—a song heralding a brighter time.

Whereas previously our moods seemed simply sad with occasional patches of light, now we may find an unsettling variety in our feelings, as happy times seem engrossing and satisfying, and then we are plunged into sadness again. Perhaps we can learn to accept these mood swings, recognizing the reality of each, knowing light gives way to darkness and darkness to light.

—MARTHA WHITMORE HICKMAN

When we begin to feel better we enter a new range of feelings, maybe even some guilt—How could I feel good when the one I loved is gone? But even when we succeed in putting that false monster aside, the mood fluctuation can be unsettling. We'll be having a genuinely wonderful time, freed at last from that continual background music of sadness. Then we remember, and it feels like dropping through a trapdoor—a much more sudden and upsetting shift than when sadness was our prevailing mood.

This is all part of our healing process. Just as a physical wound has its painful and pain-free moments, so does this wound of loss. At least we know we're moving in the right direction.

I will revel in the times I can be happy—which is what my loved one would want for me.

MARCH 7

I do not believe that sheer suffering teaches. If suffering alone taught, all the world would be wise, since everyone suffers. To suffering must be added mourning, understanding, patience, love, openness, and the willingness to remain vulnerable.

—ANNE MORROW LINDBERGH

We know this journey well—the struggle to learn from our life experiences. We are understandably wary. The suggestion that hidden in this grief is some redeeming feature—such as that we might "learn something"—is an offense to us. It is as though we are supposed not to mind so much that our hearts are broken.

But after a time, if we are fortunate and if we work at it, we begin to see that we are, in fact, stronger, more mature. This is hard work and often every impulse in our psyche fights against it, because to learn from grief seems like sanctioning what has happened.

But we are, almost in spite of ourselves, feeling better. We have made the journey from a world that was into a world that is, and as with all journeys, it has required commitment, initiative, adaptability, the willingness to give and receive help.

As I walk this walk of recovery, I will take my time. I will be alert to the road signs. I will watch for other travelers of the way who may need my help, as I need theirs.

'Tis better to have loved and lost
Than never to have loved at all.

—ALFRED TENNYSON

These lines are often used to refer to lovers, but they speak to all of us who have lost someone we loved.

A father whose daughter had died said to his pastor, "We'd rather have had her for those years than not at all, but there was a while when grief took over."

Those of us who have been through the experience of sudden, untimely death can relate to both parts of that statement. Of course we could not wish the child had never lived. But there is a time when the pain is all we know.

Yet even when the pain is most severe, we know we would never exchange our life for another's. A dear friend and mentor, who had had a distinguished career but had never had children, wrote to me after our daughter's death. Along with her condolences and shared sadness, she wrote, "Some people never have that much to lose." I couldn't help thinking she was talking about herself, and the grief I felt for her at that moment made me aware again of how much I had been given.

Even in my pain, I hold close to my heart the gift of my loved one's life.

MARCH 9

After the dead are buried, and the maimed have left the hospitals and started their new lives, after the physical pain of grief has become, with time, a permanent wound in the soul, a sorrow that will last as long as the body does, after the horrors become nightmares and sudden daylight memories, then comes the transcendent and common bond of human suffering, and with that comes forgiveness, and with forgiveness comes love.

—ANDRE DUBUS

A grieving father said, after his daughter's sudden death in an accident, "I feel as though I have joined the human family."

This sense of solidarity with the human community, of empathy and mutual love, is a hard-won bond. But in the face of tragedy—whatever its nature—one could wish for no finer resolution among human beings than that they should turn their grief into love and understanding of one another.

I don't mean to be glib about the cost of this. But let's not turn away from the great gifts of forgiveness and love that, after a long struggle, rise out of the shadows to put their arms around us, even us.

My heart lifts, in solidarity and longing, toward all who have suffered as I have. May we find and uphold one another.

For certain is death for the born
And certain is birth for the dead;
Therefore over the inevitable
Thou shouldst not grieve.

—BHAGAVAD GITA

There is a certain tranquility in this passage from Hindu Scripture, but for most of us it suggests a kind of acceptance we're not ready for yet.

The concept of reincarnation, a tenet of Hindu belief, is comforting and disquieting both—which is nothing new for religious concepts! It is comforting in that it assures the survival of the soul and its journey to ultimate perfection. It is disquieting in that it makes no promise to return our lost loved one to the circle of our friends and family, either in this life or in a future life. What we want is not a new life with new people, but a life with our own particular, longed-for loved one!

And even if we believe without a doubt that we will be reunited with our loved one, do we not grieve over the separation now? Of course.

Yet as we sweep the world and the religions of the world for comfort and insight, the peace in these words can calm our souls.

I am grateful for all words that address my need.

March 11

We are called to be food and drink for one another.
—Wendy M. Wright

That's how important we are to each other—as essential as food and water. And especially now, when we are suffering from loss.

We need our friends and family to comfort us, to buffer against loneliness, to share our memories and our grief.

And they need us—to continue to love them, to let them know we have not cut them off as we work our way through our sorrow, to be attentive, as we are able, to the ongoing needs in their lives.

And it isn't automatic, that these bonds of love and friendship will be honored. Especially when we are feeling sad, it may seem easier to isolate ourselves.

But that will not do. It isn't good for anyone. The nourishment we need to live fully comes not only from food and drink, but from the people we love and who love us.

I will not allow my sorrow to be a barrier between me and the people I love. Sometimes it may even be a bridge.

The present crisis is always the worst crisis.
—ELAINE M. PREVALLET

We get through one terrible day. Then another. Eventually the first anguish of grief begins to fade. Maybe we think we have passed the worst of it. Then something will happen—the strains of a familiar song, the scent of flowers or perfume, the figure of a stranger across the street who holds her head in that familiar way—and we are overwhelmed with fresh grief.

Things will get better. But we are always open to new recall, new occasions that remind us of our loss. Our grief seems fresh again, but it, too, will pass.

May I accept the rhythms of grieving. I have enough to worry about without scolding myself that I'm still so vulnerable.

March 13

Was ever grief like mine?

—George Herbert

Perhaps initially this is what we all think—that we are alone in experiencing so intense and painful a grief. We may even be jealous of that grief—offended at the notion that anyone else could grieve as much as we do.

And in a way we are right; our experience is like no one else's. Perhaps this holding on to our grief as though it were unique is a way of learning it, of turning it around and around until we somehow get used to the unthinkable.

Then, after a while, we may welcome the company of others. Most communities have grief support groups of one sort or another—people with whom one can speak freely of how bad it is without fear of being thought excessive or indulgent. When you begin to describe a particularly sharp moment of unexpected pain, these friends will nod their heads—*Yes, I know what you mean.* They know the stumbling blocks and pitfalls of the journey we are making, and they help by assuring us that things really do get better.

In time we become such helpers ourselves.

My grief is mine, and I am a part of the human family.

Definite work is not always that which is cut and squared for us, but that which comes as a claim upon the conscience, whether it's nursing in a hospital, or hemming a handkerchief.

—ELIZABETH M. SEWELL

When we are recovering from grief, sometimes everything seems too much trouble, every task too heavy to undertake. So we are stuck, doing nothing, waiting for some Big Project or Big Event to call us out of our lethargy.

But maybe no such summons will occur. Or if it does, it may be too much for us to take on.

The important thing is to pay attention to the small nudges we receive—some simple thing I might enjoy doing today, some minor project that might seem worthwhile. Anything to get the ball of activity rolling again. This is no time to be figuring out one's Lifework. This is a time to follow up on the small urgings, like calling a friend, clearing a few feet of the garden, or mailing a package, even returning a book to the library. Anything to establish ourselves as people who can take initiative.

Today, I will listen for a hint of something new I might do. And do it.

MARCH 15

The strands are all there: to the memory nothing is ever lost.

—EUDORA WELTY

When we have lost a loved one, we often experience a kind of generalized fear. Our life has been so shaken. Is anything secure? What else could be taken away?

One of the fears may well be, Will we forget? Will the memory of the life we have shared also slip away without the reinforcement of the person's presence, and the shared conversations about past times?

The shock of loss may for a time take away some of the kinder, more joyous memories—or make them too painful to remember. But as we begin to feel better—not so weighted with grief—the empty spaces in the patchwork quilt of memory will begin to fill in again. It will be like finding a lost treasure—the more valuable because it slipped from sight for a while.

Memories of the life I shared with my loved one are stored in my brain. What I need I will find.

It is a sad weakness in us, after all, that the thought of a man's death hallows him anew to us; as if life were not sacred, too.

—GEORGE ELIOT

There is a way in which, of course, we hallow the dead. Their lives, now over, stand in stark relief. Death is a time for solemn remembrance, for holding our loved ones at the center of attention, to acknowledge our loss and how much we shall miss them.

But it is also possible to be so preoccupied with the dead that we neglect the living. This is a particular danger when there are young children involved. In studies done on the responses of children to death in the family, a sizable number of children reported feeling overlooked and neglected. They felt their grief was not acknowledged or attended to. This is understandable but unfortunate, and probably easily avoided with a little more sensitivity to how they're feeling, along with assuring that they feel included in the family's grief. It is no favor to children—or to anyone close in the family—to try to "spare" them by keeping them at a distance. They—and all of us—need hugs and reassurance more than protection.

There is a fine balance between attending to my own needs and being mindful of the needs of the living, who may depend on me for comfort and reassurance.

March 17

Every aspect of life had become perilous to Dinah, and all she knew how to do was to hang on to her life exactly as it was, to let routine and necessity direct her days.
—ROBB FORMAN DEW

One effect of losing a loved one, particularly if death is sudden and unexpected, is that we become newly aware of the fragility of life. If this tragedy can befall us, what next? We can become fearful, almost paranoid. A mother whose child was killed in an auto accident tells me she cannot bear to have her other child come home later than she expected. "Call me if you're going to be late. Even ten minutes. Please," she tells him.

Our security in the world is threatened. Our inner lives are in turmoil. To follow methodically the patterns of the day may give us some sense of order so we will not break apart.

Beyond that, we may feel that by sticking to our established ways, perhaps we will keep the fates from noticing us and be spared further unexpected terror. These are primal, irrational fears—but the loss we have gone through is not rational, either.

Later—not now—we'll have the energy and courage to cope with change.

I will live through these days the best I can, trusting that in time my spontaneity and energy will return.

Love . . . bears all things, believes all things, hopes all things, endures all things. Love never ends.

—I CORINTHIANS 13:7–8

What a truckload of responsibility and potential for pain we take on when we love another human being: all the dangers of misunderstanding, of betrayal, of indifference, and ultimately, of loss.

To more than balance those dangers, we feel the possibility of life made rich through sharing experiences with another—of physical and spiritual warmth and communion, of enriched understanding and common achievement, of a stay against loneliness and isolation.

Most of us have no trouble opting for love.

But then, to have invested so much of our life's energy in the life of a loved one—and then to find that loved one gone! Is it any wonder we are, for a time, laid low?

But the love we have shared helps form the strength to deal with loss. The hope and joy we have known help us believe in the possibility of hope and joy again.

And the intensity of grief (which *will* moderate, though we may find that hard to believe) mirrors the intensity of shared love, which will continue to beam through our life, to illumine and nourish all that we do and are.

Love never ends. Never.

MARCH 19

What was it in the sweep of the sky, the giant outcropping of rock, the sassafras leaf in my hand? I did not know, but I felt hushed by awe and a quiet joy.

—AVERY BROOKE

Perhaps we all have our special places of healing. In a class I took on "Art as Meditation," the leader suggested, "Close your eyes. Think of your favorite place in all the world."

Where is yours? Where is mine? Perhaps they are different places at different times. But as grievers, we would do well to go, as often as we're able, to places that have a healing calm for us.

And maybe it's not a single specific place, but a type of place. A friend of mine says, "The ocean. Anywhere, so long as it's the ocean."

Once there, we have to be willing to let the place speak to us, and to open our hearts, to "the sweep of sky, the outcropping of rock"—to the peace that seems to emanate from such places, telling us in some mysterious way that all shall be well.

In communion with the beauty of nature, I find an affirmation of all that is, including me.

The plant grows in the mist and under clouds as truly as under sunshine.

—WILLIAM ELLERY CHANNING

After a traumatic event such as the loss of a loved one, we may feel as though our life has stopped. Nothing can go forward after this. What sense can we make of the rest of our life?

Fortunately, life will pull us along, whether or not we give it our blessing. And one day, like a storm that passes, we will see light again, and realize that during all the time we felt lost in darkness and confusion, processes of healing and growth were doing their slow and often silent work. We have not lost time at all, but like the seed that has lain apparently inert in the ground all winter and now is ready to begin its springtime dance, we have been moved along in steady and unseen ways into new life. Like the butterfly emerging from the cocoon after a long darkness, we will shake caterpillar dust from our wings and realize we can fly.

Sometimes I feel frozen in place, as though I will never move or grow again. But all the time, One who is higher than I is leading me through this dark land.

MARCH 21

Ah woe is me! Winter is come and gone,
But grief returns with the revolving year.
—PERCY BYSSHE SHELLEY

Anniversaries! They continue to plague us. Each holiday, the remembrance of what we "used to do"—the spring picnics, the Easter trip, the local fireworks show on the Fourth of July, the family gathering at Thanksgiving. And then, of course, the private anniversaries—birthdays, wedding anniversaries, the anniversary of the day of death.

Sometimes we forget. And then wonder, by midafternoon, why we are feeling so low—until we look at the calendar and remember. The conscious mind may forget, but the unconscious has a longer memory.

Over time it will get easier. But it's well to be mindful of anniversaries and realize that on some level we will remember and probably be sad.

So acknowledge—This is the day. Perhaps tell an understanding friend. And then—be a little kind to yourself. Perhaps plan some diverting activity. No need to mourn all day. Your loved one wouldn't want that. You won't forget. Next year will come around . . .

I will be free to turn away from my grief when I can. Life is not an endurance test.

I think I am beginning to understand why grief feels so much like suspense. It comes from the frustration of so many impulses that have become habitual . . . I keep on through habit fitting an arrow to the string; then I remember and have to lay the bow down.

—C. S. LEWIS

In the first days, weeks, and months, the loss feels like an amputation. The nerves twinge as though the limb were still there. Particularly if death has come suddenly, these involuntary impulses occur. We start to set the old number of places at the table. We count over one too many seats at the movies. Each time we catch ourselves it jabs like a needle in the heart.

But after a time—a long time—we may welcome the association as a poignant reminder of happy times shared and not to be forgotten. I recall returning home after the death of my daughter and saying to my son, "How can I live in this house? I'll see her everywhere."

He said, "There may come a time when you'll be glad."

Now, years later, as I walk through the rooms where she lived with us, I welcome those associations.

Healing moves at its own pace. What is a burden one day may be a gift another day.

March 23

Let not future things disturb thee, for thou wilt come to
them, if it shall be necessary, having with thee the same
reason which thou now usest for present things.
—Marcus Antoninus

One of the difficulties we grievers have to contend with is
anticipating all those future occasions when we shall be
without our loved one.

What is accomplished by anticipating this anguish?
Nothing. We can't foresee which troubles will beset us,
and even if we could, are we so eager for them that we
want them for company long in advance?

Do we think we won't have then the ability we have
now—to deal with a crisis? Presumably we'll be at least
as able then as we are now and we'll know what to do.

Why not deal with the events and uncertainties of this
day?

◆◆

*I will stay with the anxieties and cares of today, trusting to the
unknown future its unknown cares.*

A person that never climbs will never fall.

—WILLIAM SHAKESPEARE

Sometimes, devastated as we are by grief at the loss of a loved one, we may wonder, Is it worth it? Would it be wiser not to be so invested in people that when they die we feel our own world is all but destroyed?

We know the answer. Such a choice would deny what is most richly human in our experience—the ability to make close and intense connections with other human beings.

No more could a parent keep a child from engaging in any pursuit that might involve danger. Of course for children as for adults, there are some pursuits that are so dangerous only the foolhardy are drawn to them, just as there are some relationships so dangerous we enter them at our peril.

Our life choices waver back and forth across the thin line of unwise involvement on one side and rich human exchange on the other. It is a matter calling for wise judgment—to whom we entrust our heart. But to hold back from loving and being loved because there is always the danger of losing is like trying to prevent a child from learning to walk because the child might fall. The child will fall—and will get up and walk again.

The risks of loving are worth taking, even the risk of loss.

MARCH 25

It has been well said that no man ever sank under the burden of the day. It is when tomorrow's burden is added to the burden of today that the weight is more than a man can bear. Never load yourselves so, my friends.

—GEORGE MACDONALD

How can we *not* look ahead to all those days, months, and years when we will be without the one we loved?

There are times, surely, when we can't help ourselves. But we don't have to do it all the time. Perhaps we can adopt the pattern recommended in the "rational-emotive" approach.

Allow ourselves a certain half hour of the day when we will give our grief full sway—and even allow ourselves to anticipate the long future without our loved one. At other times, when those thoughts come knocking, we turn them away—*Not now, this isn't the time for you. Come back at five-thirty—then you can have my full attention.*

When five-thirty comes, we should be as good as our word: if those sad thoughts come rolling in, let them. When the half hour is up, inwardly change the subject and busy yourself with something else.

I am not trying to overlook these feelings of long-term grief—just to keep my life from being inundated by them.

If you are an artist, it is work that fulfills and makes you come into wholeness, and that goes on through a lifetime. Whatever the wounds that have to heal, the moment of creation assures that all is well, that one is still in tune with the universe, that the inner chaos can be proved and distilled into order and beauty.

—MAY SARTON

May Sarton was speaking as a writer. But there are all kinds of ways in which all of us make art in our lives—a splendid photograph, a needlepoint pillow, a meal, a garden, the arrangement of a room. The important thing is making something: taking words, colors, pieces of wood, seeds, or food and arranging them in a meaningful and beautiful way. In doing this we are showing ourselves that we are not undone by the disorder our grief has cast us into. See—we can take this, even this, and weave it into our life's fabric.

So take a step. Make something. Perhaps something like a poem or a painting can express your grief. Maybe a meal, or a sweater, is more your style. A friend whose son had committed suicide tells me that when she started to sew some clothes for herself, she began to believe in life again.

Perhaps in some new work of my hands I will find solace and meaning for my life.

When your burden is heaviest, you can always lighten a little some other burden. At the times when you cannot see God, there is still open to you this sacred possibility, to *show* God; for it is the love and kindness of human hearts through which the divine reality comes home to men, whether they name it or not. Let this thought, then, stay with you: there may be times when you cannot find help, but there is no time when you cannot give help.

—GEORGE S. MERRIAM

Often, especially in first grief, we don't have the will or energy to do anything much, for ourselves or for anyone else. But as we begin to get better, we can give ourselves a welcome break from our preoccupying sadness by doing something for another. It expresses the hope that we are not always going to be stuck in this valley of sadness. Not to mention that such a move on our part can be reassuring and useful to someone else!

It is amazing the way depression lifts when we are able to move out of our own concerns and do something for someone else.

Grief comes in unexpected surges . . . Mysterious cues that set off a reminder of grief. It comes crashing like a wave, sweeping me in its crest, twisting me inside out. Then recedes, leaving me broken. Oh, Mama, I don't want to eat, to walk, to get out of bed. Reading, working, cooking, listening, mothering. Nothing matters. I do not want to be distracted from my grief. I wouldn't mind dying. I wouldn't mind at all.

—TOBY TALBOT

Anything can set us off—a fragment of music, a piece of old clothing we come upon when cleaning out a closet, a slip of paper that falls out of a book, with that familiar handwriting on it. Just when we thought we were feeling better, gaining some stability, something comes to plunge us right back into that raw, overpowering sense of loss.

Not only are we unable to think of anything else, we don't want to. There is nothing on the horizon but this. Our grief occupies our life out to the edges. If we try to look to the future, our glance is stuck in this mire of grief. Is it any wonder we think of our own death as not such a bad idea?

This mood comes without warning and it is devastating. It also passes. So . . . live in your grief, yes. But also wait.

To accept the surges of grief when they come is also to know they will pass.

MARCH 29

Be patient with everyone, but above all with yourself. I mean, do not be disturbed because of your imperfections, and always rise up bravely from a fall. I'm glad that you make daily a new beginning; there is no better means of progress in the spiritual life than to be continually beginning afresh.

—FRANCIS DE SALES

One of the things that is so hard about recovering from grief is that it Takes So Long. And we get discouraged, not only from the continuing presence of the grief, but because of our own inability to handle it better. Just when we think we are making progress—wham, it sweeps over us and seems new again.

Nowhere more than here is it important to be patient with ourselves, not let ourselves be weighed down by the discouragements of yesterday. Each day is a new day, a fresh beginning.

◆◆

As I stand on the threshold of this day, I leave behind me the cares and anxieties of yesterday.

Possess yourself as much as you possibly can in peace;
not by any effort, but by letting all things fall to the ground
which trouble or excite you. This is no work, but is, as it
were, a setting down a fluid to settle that has become
turbid through agitation.

—MADAME GUYON

This is another way of suggesting that we try to live in the
moment and not let preoccupation with our grief take over
the rest of our life. It is easier said than done—putting our
sadness aside and paying attention only to what is happening around us now. It is a counsel we will not always
be able to follow, and probably shouldn't try to. But the
image of letting all things fall to the ground is a good one
and a mental exercise worth trying.

So imagine that you are standing still and straight, and
that by a touch of an inner-control button you let all the
stress and grief in your life slowly start slipping down
your arms and legs, to be absorbed into the ground beneath you. How much lighter you feel! Your arms could
almost rise into the air—so free are they from the weight
of all that remembered pain.

Think you have gotten rid of it all? Walk away a few
steps and try the same exercise again.

*To some extent it is in my power to decide when I will let grief
take over.*

MARCH 31

> They that love beyond the world cannot be separated by
> it. Death is but crossing the world, as friends do the seas;
> they live in one another still.
>
> —WILLIAM PENN

This analogy of friends being separated by the breadth of
the sea and yet living in one another strikes us as apt—
and hopeful—as we consider the mystery of death.

After all, was our love ever dependent on the immediate
physical world around us? Were we not somehow "in
touch" with one another even though we might be a thousand miles apart.

To be sure, the death of the physical body is entirely
different from being somewhere on the other side of the
world! We cannot minimize the wrenching deprivation we
experience when our loved one dies. But in the ways in
which our love was "beyond the world"—not dependent
on a particular place or time or set of circumstances—
surely that love persists, wherever we are, whatever the
circumstances of our life now.

*As I cherish my friends who are far away, I hold in my heart
the memory of my loved one.*

Because humor brings us back to earth, it helps us to use well what is left to us even when we are keenly aware of what we have lost or been denied. Only those who know how to weep can also laugh heartily.
—KATHLEEN R. FISCHER

We are all familiar with those two line drawings for the theater: the comic face, the tragic face. We know well that both comedy and tragedy are part of human life.

We hear the phrase "comic relief"—unexpected humor when the situation seems grim.

How does all this come to us when we are in the throes of our own grief?

At first it may seem that nothing can ever be funny again. Then we may find to our surprise that we are more appreciative of humor, not less, than those who are presently untouched by grief.

Are we startled? Do we think it "unseemly"—this laughter that erupts from us in the midst of sadness?

But when we are down, comic relief is most needed—as a starving person craves food more than one who is well fed. Our laughter is a safety valve against being inundated by grief, a vote of confidence that we won't be floored by this event, sad though we may be.

Sometimes laughter is the best medicine.

APRIL 2

The deadliest of all things to me is my loss of faith in nature. No spring—no summer. Fog always, and the snow faded from the Alps.

—JOHN RUSKIN

This kind of pervasive depression is certainly what life feels like often, when we are living in the wake of grievous loss. It's as though we're standing still. If our own life will not move in the way we had wanted, we're unwilling that anything else move in its accustomed way, either. We even resent that night and day follow each other without taking note of our anguish. How can they act out "business as usual" when our private world is in such chaos?

It's probably unavoidable, after the first rush of grief and crisis, that from time to time we hold the world, the seasons, the days and nights, at arm's length—a kind of general anesthesia against life, because it is so painful to allow ourselves to feel.

Then, bit by bit, the nerve endings begin to tingle again. We are, perhaps against our will, jarred into an awareness of life around us. We are aware again that it is beautiful, and that we can take pleasure and nourishment from the world, even though our loved one has moved on.

My life is what I am given now. I will trust that the fog will lift and the mountains will be beautiful once more.

A faithful friend is the medicine of life.

—THE APOCRYPHA

During the week following the memorial service for our daughter, a friend called me every morning. She was taking her teenage son to basketball camp a half hour's drive into the country and asked if I would like to ride along.

I was hesitant. I hadn't known this friend for very long. I knew she would encourage me to talk. Did I really want to? Would I be so overwrought that I'd embarrass myself?

It was a risk for me—as it was for her to invite me. But I went—the first day, and then each day throughout the week.

Our rides to camp with her son were mostly quiet. But on the way back we would often stop at the park, get a drink of something, and sit under a tree for a while. I talked, and talked, and cried, and talked. About what? About the feeling of loss, the day's trivia, the rest of the family, the unfinished business with my daughter.

They were emotional times, of course, filled with articulated pain. But each day as she dropped me off at my house, I felt better, able to go on. The pressure was released once more—as steam is released when the lid is lifted from a boiling pot. It was as elemental, as simple, as incontrovertible, as that.

◆◆

Friends can help keep the flow of grief moving.

April 4

Faith is the centerpiece of a connected life. It allows us to live by the grace of invisible strands. It is a belief in a wisdom superior to our own. Faith becomes a teacher in the absence of fact.

—Terry Tempest Williams

We would like to *know*, wouldn't we? Or think we would. Experiences like the loss of a loved one fill our lives with questions about the nature of life beyond death. What is the nature of God? What will be our experience of God—and our loved one—after we ourselves die?

Of course these are unanswerable questions. But we have to do something with our longing to know, with our yearning to continue a relationship with our loved one.

Blessed are those for whom faith can absorb the shock of not knowing, who can trust in "a wisdom superior to our own," in "the grace of invisible strands."

Perhaps all of us, whatever our faith tradition, can extend our sense of trust into the unknown world. Perhaps it seems a risk. But it may help us profoundly. And—unlike some risks—it won't do us any harm!

Unknowing, I will trust the unknown.

One of the most pathetic things about us human beings is our touching belief that there are times when the truth is not good enough for us; that it can and must be improved upon. We have to be utterly broken before we can realize that it is impossible to better the truth. It is the truth that we deny which so tenderly and forgivingly picks up the fragments and puts them together again.

—LAURENS VAN DER POST

We do our best, trying to change what has happened. We play our games of What if . . . "What if we hadn't gone to that resort and what if we had planned some other outing so she wouldn't have gone horseback riding?" "What if we'd urged him to have a checkup sooner?" "What if she'd never started smoking?" "What if we'd stopped him from driving when he'd been drinking?" It is self-torture and we know it, but we can't seem to stop rearranging the facts to make the reality come out better.

And in the meantime, the world we cannot change waits patiently to welcome us back. It waits as a parent waits for a child to vent anger and frustration when the block building has fallen down or a playmate has acted cruelly. Then is the time for comfort, for reassurance and a hug, and for consideration of what to do now.

◆◆

I know the truth always wins. Someday I may be able to step away from the battle.

APRIL 6

The other Sunday, I remember, in a political discussion I said some things I shouldn't have. I can't tell you how unhappy I am about it now. It seems as though I had been harsh with someone no longer able to defend himself . . . These are things I can't yet bear to think about. They cause me so much grief. Life has started again. If only I had an aim, an ambition of any kind, it would help me to bear it. But that isn't the case.

—MARCEL PROUST

How we berate ourselves! Conversations in which we feel we weren't as kind as we might have been stick in our minds. We torture ourselves, wishing we could take back our words. And because we are so debilitated with grief that we cannot muster the energy to internally "change the subject" and get on with something else, these grievances against ourselves continue to sound in our minds.

Chances are that this incident (and others) which we remember with such chagrin was nowhere near as big an "event" in the life of our loved one as it has become in ours. Of course we have said hurtful things to people we love—and will probably continue to do so. Think of it as the price of a spontaneous relationship. Would you really like to have everything that's said to you weighed solemnly for all its possible negative effects?

Our loved ones forgive us, as we forgive them.

Spirituality in its broadest sense is, quite simply, a way of
life that reveals an awareness of the sacred and a relationship with the Holy One in the midst of our human
frailty, brokenness and limitations.

—EDWARD C. SELLNER

To be faced with the loss of a loved one is to be engaged—
or reengaged more intensely—with the experience of the
spiritual. Questions of our loved one's survival, of our
own relationship to the spiritual world, of our possible
communion with the dead now or after our own death—
all come to us with new urgency.

Surely if we can summon an awareness of the Holy One
as a loving, caring reality, we shall be miles ahead! We
can bear the uncertainty of answers to our questions if we
feel that the One who is in charge cares for us all, grieves
with us when we are sad, and wills our good. This has
been the yearning, and the confidence, of believers
through the ages.

"Now faith is the assurance of things hoped for, the
conviction of things not seen," said the apostle Paul in the
Letter to the Hebrews. These things are no less real for
being "not seen."

*In the midst of my brokenness, O Holy One, may I be made
newly aware of You.*

Sometimes, with the best of intentions, friends don't know how to help. They may feel that to bring up the subject of our loss is to risk making us feel worse, so they avoid it and talk of other things while the presence of the unspoken builds up to an almost intolerable pressure.

—MARTHA WHITMORE HICKMAN

We are at a small gathering of friends who are chatting about their own and one another's lives—but it is as though the subject of our own loss and grief is out of bounds. Everyone knows of it, everyone cares, but no one speaks of it. And, sensing that we would be violating some unspoken taboo, neither do we.

Sound familiar? There may be times when the best recourse is to go along with casual conversation, surviving as best we can. But sometimes, if these are close friends, it's best to break the bubble of camouflage and say, "I need to talk about what's going on with me."

Usually the tension will break, there will be an immediate sense of support, and relief, and the question "How are you?" will be a real invitation to tell the truth. We will feel the tension of unexpressed grief move—figuratively, at least—from our body into the welcoming arms of friends who love us but don't know what to do.

When I risk telling who I am, I give a gift to myself and to my friends.

I must force myself to look upon the familiar things, the coat hanging on the chair, the hat in the hall . . . To ease the pain I took over some of his things for myself. I wore his shirts, sat at his writing desk, used his pens to acknowledge the hundreds of letters of condolence; and by the very process of identification with the objects he had touched, felt the closer to him.

—DAPHNE DU MAURIER

What to do about the *things?* For some people they are a comfort, an aid to healing. For others, to dwell upon the objects associated with the loved one is to be caught in a vise of anguishing memory and pain.

Each of us has to find his or her own way. Try something, and if that doesn't work, try something else. When our daughter died, we quickly gave away most of her clothes—some to particular friends, some to a charity organization. But we saved a few, putting them away in a drawer so we could see them if we wanted, but weren't face-to-face with them all the time. We saved some things to give away as occasions arose—a jewelry box with her name to go later to another loved child of the same name, a British coin to wear in someone else's wedding shoe. Some we kept, and the comfort and pleasure they bring grow as the pain of her not-being-here has become softer, more mellow.

I can take my time, disposing of the things as I am ready.

April 10

At every point in the human journey we find that we have to let go in order to move forward; and letting go means dying a little. In the process we are being created anew, awakened afresh to the source of our being.
—Kathleen R. Fischer

We know full well that our loved one has died. Do we recognize that in that death a part of us has died, too?

The part of us that lived in our relationship to that person alive in the world has died.

The part of us that lived in expectation of a future on earth together has died.

The part of us that enjoyed the commonality of shared memories has died.

This is a lot to lose, and perhaps it will be easier to accept the effects of our loved one's dying if we acknowledge the profound event this is in our life, too.

If we cannot let go, then our lives will be burdened with spots of unresolved death, and our whole system poisoned.

But if we can, then in the spaces where those deaths have occurred, new life will spring. "Nature abhors a vacuum," we have heard many times. Some of the new life may be our new relationship with our lost love. But we will have to let go first.

I will open my hand and heart, to relinquish. And to receive.

What is essential does not die but clarifies.
—THORNTON WILDER

One of the ways we can enrich our lives after a great loss is to sink ourselves in the study of that loved one's past. Now that he or she is no longer with us in the physical sense, we begin to understand in a new way the life of the one we love who has died. What were the silent spaces in that life like? Perhaps we can only conjecture, using our understanding of the person and what little we may know of particular periods in his or her life. But we can sit quietly and let our imagination play. What was that person's early childhood like? Are there old photos? Old mementos? What can they tell us? Why was this particular handkerchief saved, this bunch of dried flowers?

While our memory of the person and the stories he or she told us are still fresh, are there things we could write down to preserve those stories for the person's descendants? A dear friend whose brother died wrote for his children an account of her years growing up with this beloved brother. What a treasured gift for them! And what a cherished journey of remembrance for her.

It is a wonderful and astonishing comfort to rediscover my lost love.

APRIL 12

I have been thinking about the change of the seasons. I don't want to miss spring this year. I want to be there on the spot the moment the grass turns green.

—ANNIE DILLARD

Grief is preoccupying. For a while it seems to take all our attention. We forget what day it is—or don't care. We stop attending to public issues in which we have been involved. We may forget appointments, or whom we have seen and under what circumstances.

At first this is inevitable—and appropriate. We need to immerse ourselves in this shocking new world until we, in some sense, "get used to it"—as swimmers diving into cold water swim vigorously around until they grow accustomed to the temperature.

But we need to be careful. Because we are missing things, too. Perhaps we need to make a conscious effort to begin to pay attention to what is happening beyond the pain of this grief.

Because we wouldn't want to miss the grass turning green, or the smell of wisteria, or the sound of children laughing.

Things other than my grief are going on in the world. Let me pay attention so I don't miss what could help me heal.

Was he still hovering about the house at home, the essence of himself, and were I there would I perceive his presence? . . . I fought off the mighty yearning to go in search of him, wherever he was. For surely he was looking for me, too. We were ill at ease, always, when apart. But where are the pathways?

—PEARL BUCK

This quandary presents itself to all who have lost loved ones. My mother, months after my father's death, said to me, "He must be *somewhere* where I can find him."

A year later, I, looking up into a starlit night soon after my daughter's death, thought—Maybe that's where she is, up there among the stars.

In some ways these are heartbreaking conjectures, because there are no answers, no destinations this side of death to which we can travel to find our lost love.

Yet sometimes we do feel his or her spirit hovering near. Whether it is our own projection or, in some way, the visiting spirit of our loved one, we have no way of knowing. We would like it to be our loved one—some contact, some assurance of continuing life. But oddly enough, perhaps it doesn't matter a great deal. If we are comforted, let's be grateful for that. And if this easing of the spirit comes from our own imagination—well, the Creator of life gave us our imagination, too.

I will be open to the ways my love and I care for each other.

April 14

So do not worry about tomorrow, for tomorrow will bring worries of its own. Today's trouble is enough for today.
—Matthew 6:34

Easier said than done, especially if our whole life has been shaken by loss. How are we *not* going to look toward the future without some degree of worry? How am I going to get through the rest of my life without the one I have lost?

It is all very well to urge that we trust our future to God, that we acknowledge the futility of worry and just quit cold turkey. It's a matter of basic faith. It's just common sense.

But as we know, common sense isn't all that common. And faith may need its props, its frames of reference.

Someone has suggested we try to live our lives in "daytight" compartments, as though a wall were dropped on either side of this twenty-four-hour stretch of time. Not a bad idea!

I know that worry is useless and a waste of time. I will try, today, to put down a clump of worry, leave it, and walk away.

Suffering breaks our world. Like a tree struck by lightning—splintered, shaken, denuded—our world is broken by suffering, and we will never be the same again. What will become of us is a mystery.

—NATHAN KOLLAR

Any major event in our lives affects every other aspect of our lives—as a stone tossed into a stream creates ripples that extend all the way to the shore.

And often we don't know what's "out there," or how we're going to be affected by this change somewhere down the line.

Under the calmest of circumstances there is no planning that can anticipate every contingency. But when our lives are all but shattered by grief, it is often a mystery how we're going to get through the next twenty-four hours, let alone make the necessary adaptations for the next five years, or ten, or twenty.

There is no hurry. And no hurrying. The future will unfold, whether we're ready or not. We will make what impact we can on that future. Much of it will be out of our hands—a mystery, then as now.

Part of the adventure of my life is—I don't know all that I may become.

April 16

At a time like this, how beautiful is every human face.
—News Commentator

The occasion was the death of Robert Kennedy, and the newsman was watching the long line of mourners slowly moving by Kennedy's body as it lay in state.

I think of this quote again as a camera plays over another crowd, this time at a political convention. The speaker is talking about her experience of contracting the AIDS virus through a blood transfusion, and of the subsequent death of the son to whom she later gave birth. The crowd is hushed. People watch with tears in their eyes—no hint of the stridency and competitiveness that have colored this convention and will again.

Perhaps these two scenes remind us that as we confront death, there is a reservoir of love and compassion in the human community. We don't need to be afraid to show our vulnerability, because to mourn when we are bereaved is not a sign of weakness but a stepping into the circle where all the brothers and the sisters can put their arms around us and hold us close, if we give them a chance.

The love inherent in the human family is available to me.

Speak to the earth, and it shall teach thee.

—JOB 12:8

In the spring, when all the world awakens, sometimes our loss seems most unbearable. New life is evident everywhere—a great stirring in the earth after the long, bleak winter. And we? The same dull fact of death lies heavy on our hearts, made even heavier by contrast with the beauty all around us—the first crocus, the daffodils, the fingered glory of redbud trees. Winter is more akin to our mood than this!

But is it? Can we try, even a little bit, to *believe in* spring? To believe in its witness to the economy of creation—that nothing is lost, nothing is wasted? And that our loved one, too, is transformed into new life? If we can believe that, then the abundance we see around us can give us courage and hope, as well as a nourishing feast for our senses, here and now.

May each glimpse of the returning flowers in spring be like a conversation with my loved one.

April 18

When I put the key into the apartment door I had a moment of panic and stood hesitatingly on the doorstep, until I felt clearly a "Welcome home" emanating from inside. The sun was shining and a neighbor, who had heard me come in, called out to offer a cup of tea. In spite of the emptiness and the sense of desolation, it was a homecoming and the beginning of a new life.

—LILY PINCUS

How hard it is to reenter the accustomed world when a loved one has gone. The empty space is much more conspicuous than if one were to go to a strange land. Our son, returning from college, found his sister's loss much more consuming of his energy than when he was away at school. That landscape had never contained her. But *this* was where he had known her, been with her day by day, year after year.

Yet we must face down our demons and reenter these accustomed places of our daily lives, or we will never incorporate this event into our lives.

There is a sense of achievement, too, of having gone down to the bone, faced the worst. This is where our life together took place. This is where our accommodation to the truth must be made. Then we can begin to rebuild.

I will enter the hallowed places of my life resolutely, and without fear.

Who would have thought my shrivel'd heart
Could have recovered greenness?

—GEORGE HERBERT

Springtime after the cold and darkness of winter is no more startling than the return of hope and light to the heart of the mourner.

When the loss first hit us, it was hard to look ahead at all. When we did, we saw nothing but bleakness and the continuing specter of absence. Maybe we were *told* the worst of this would pass, and in a sense we knew that to be true, because we had seen it happen with other people who had suffered loss. But being told or even observing from a distance is one thing, and believing is another.

Then, as with the first shoot of a crocus or a daffodil, and the first green budding of trees, the picture changes! The climate of our life has altered. Our grief is still there, as there are vestiges of winter visible in spring, but new hope has broken through, the bright hours grow longer, and we take delight in life again. There will still be many days when cold grips the heart, but we have begun to reenter some seasons of joy. Who would have thought?

◆◆

Let me relish the first stirrings of new life in myself—as welcome as the flowers in spring.

APRIL 20

Grief fills the room up of my absent child,
Lies in his bed, walks up and down with me,
Puts on his pretty looks, repeats his words,
Remembers me of all his gracious parts,
Stuffs out his vacant garments with his form.
—WILLIAM SHAKESPEARE

It needn't be a child, though that always has its extra measure of grief. Whoever it is who has gone from our life—that person's clothes, favorite things, places of habitation, keep reminding us of what we have lost.

And not only clothing, of course. There are the places we used to be together. As an adult, I spent a nostalgic day returning to a small island where, decades earlier, my grandfather had had a cabin to which my mother would take us children for magical summer weeks. For years I had avoided going there because it was so painful. Now, though I was wistful still for this beloved figure of my childhood, the pain had transmuted to an increased reverence and love for what he had been for me, a chief figure in my own "communion of saints."

The presence that makes me sad may one day make me glad.

We cannot afford to forget any experience, not even the most painful.

—DAG HAMMARSKJÖLD

Why not?

Think about it. Even to ask such a question throws into relief how our lives would be impoverished were we to forget our painful experiences.

There is an old folktale about a group of people, each of whom was given the chance to throw one trouble into a central heap in the middle of the room. Then they were invited to choose one from the pile. They each ended up taking back their own.

I suppose this seems so right to us because we know we are, each of us, the sum of our experiences, and to negate any of those experiences, even the most painful—maybe especially the most painful—is to deny not only what we have learned from those experiences, but also our very selves.

◆◆

I will embrace my life, all of it. If there are changes for the better that I can make, I will try to make them. Where I cannot, I will accept that, too. But—even if I could—I will not forget my pain. I will honor it. It is part of who I am.

APRIL 22

Joy comes from simple and natural things, mists over meadows, sunlight on leaves, the path of the moon over water. Even rain and wind and stormy clouds bring joy, just as knowing animals and flowers and where they live.
—SIGURD F. OLSON

Let us for a few moments lay aside our grieving and notice, as though nothing else existed, the world around us.

Of course, it's better to do this if you can be in a lovely place. But there are always simple things around us that could gladden our hearts if we would let them. Children rejoice in sunshine and rain, in puddles to walk through, in the way light reflects off a fragment of colored glass, in the way grass shoots up through cracks in a sidewalk. For children, the immediate world is what calls to them, brings them joy or sadness.

We carry our sadness with us for a long time. But let's not allow it to call all the shots! Let's give ourselves a break by taking note of the springtime—the way trees, flowers, and bushes seem to erupt overnight, and the days lengthen, the air grows soft, the birds come back, the rabbits reappear on the lawn.

To allow myself to revel in simple joys will ease me into new hope, new courage for my life.

. . .
The sun was warm but the wind was chill.
You know how it is with an April day
When the sun is out and the wind is still,
You're one month on in the middle of May.
But if you so much as dare to speak,
A cloud comes over the sunlit arch,
A wind comes off a frozen peak,
And you're two months back in the middle of March . . .
                                        —ROBERT FROST

So it is with the weather of grieving. One moment we'll
be feeling good, moving on in some productive activity—
or some nonproductive activity (one doesn't always have
to be productive!)—and something will happen to bring
back the grief as though it were all fresh. Maybe it's a
song, a passage in a book, a scene in a movie. Sometimes
the sheer beauty of the world can move us to tears, and
part of the poignancy of that moment is how much we
miss the one who cannot share it with us.

These sudden flashes back into intense grief will grow
farther apart. We'll get over them more quickly. But we'll
probably never be free of them—and wouldn't want to be.
They preserve for us our connection with the one we love.

As for leaps forward into happy times? I remember my
joy when I learned my first grandchild was on the way!

The ups and downs of "inner weather" are part of my healing.

APRIL 24

Injuries hurt not more in the receiving than in the remembrance. A small injury shall go as it comes; a great injury may dine or sup with me; but none at all shall lodge with me . . . Grief for things past that cannot be remedied, and care for things to come that cannot be prevented, may easily hurt, can never benefit me. I will therefore commit myself to God in both, and enjoy the present.

—JOSEPH HALL

Almost all of us have some "unfinished business" with a loved one who has died—hurts that never were resolved, questions we never got answers to, things we would like to have said but never did.

It is easy to brood over these, to torture ourselves with "if only" yearnings to somehow make it right.

Two things may help free us from these broodings. One is to realize the futility of such self-torture and decide not to give it hospitality. A second is to honor the possibility that whatever life exists beyond death, surely it is more compassionate, more understanding, more forgiving than we experience on our human plane; and that our loved one is aware of our dilemma, and all our unresolved questions are absorbed into the light of a higher truth.

I will gather all my unresolved hurts and guilt in my hand and lay them at the feet of the All-wise, the All-knowing.

Faith consists in believing when it is beyond the power of reason to believe. It is not enough that a thing be possible for it to be believed.

—VOLTAIRE

In contrast to the suggestion that faith is "believing what you know ain't so," perhaps faith is believing what there's no way of knowing whether it's so or not.

It's not a matter of faith to believe that if you mix red with blue you'll get purple, or that one and one makes two.

In our extremity of wanting to know *for sure* that our loved one . . . understood us, forgave us, is happily in Heaven, watches over us, _____ (we can each fill in our own), there is no way to know.

What is at issue is whether God, the universe, is to be trusted. That, too, is a matter of faith, and from it come all manner of subsidiary questions.

A man well schooled in theology and life says that his answer to these questions of afterlife is that whatever wonderful scenario we can imagine for life after death, God's gifts will be infinitely greater, and surprising. Not a bad conjecture when one is mulling things over. And over. And over.

Since I cannot know, I will gamble on trust.

APRIL 26

He did not say: You will not be troubled, you will not be belaboured, you will not be disquieted; but he said: You will not be overcome.

—JULIAN OF NORWICH

Sometimes we feel that we will be overcome. When we are tired, and the future looks grim and mined with occasions for potential grief, we feel as though it will be too much for us. We won't be able to "take it" anymore.

But the weeks go by and we haven't crumbled yet. We've been sad, even despairing, continuing to see the future as bleak—but we haven't been overcome.

And after a while a sturdy confidence sets in. Look what we have been through! Look what we have survived. And if we've done it so far, why not tomorrow, and next week and next month, and on those occasions which are bound to come when we feel, once again, that we may not make it through?

But look!—we have! And we can again.

I am strong. I am saddened, sometimes tired, discouraged. But I've made it so far. I will not be overcome.

Can I see another's woe,
And not be in sorrow, too?
Can I see another's grief,
And not seek for kind relief?

—WILLIAM BLAKE

One of the things grief does for us is to sensitize us to the grief of others. At first this is no particular gift: we are too aware of our own sadness to think about the sorrows of others. But sooner than we think, we will learn of people with grief like ours, and will reach out to them.

Maybe they will be people we already know. Maybe they will be strangers. But if circumstances throw us together and we have a chance to talk, we will be strangers no more. We will know immediately the suffering each other is going through and we will be mutually strengthened and uplifted in this new relationship.

This story continues. As others who know our story experience their own tragedies, they will turn to us for help, and our empathy will give them comfort and hope. We will also be reminded of how far we have come and of the commonality of the human story that enables us to love and support each other.

◆◆

I am a member of the human family and all in need are my brothers and sisters.

April 28

And time remembered is grief forgotten,
And frosts are slain and flowers begotten,
And in green underwood and cover
Blossom by blossom the spring begins.
                    —ALGERNON CHARLES SWINBURNE

Though we can scarcely believe it when our grief is new, there will come a time when what we remember will be, not the so-sorrowful occasion of death, but the rich and happy times in the life of our loved one.

It won't happen all at once, any more than winter passes in one glorious sunny day that takes away all the cold and melts the snow.

But one day, just as crocuses and daffodils appear one at a time as solitary harbingers of spring, we will find ourselves smiling (laughing, even!) as we remember our loved one. The lift of that memory is, for a while at least, far removed from the overriding sadness we've known. "Blossom by blossom," memory by memory, the spring-time returns.

Somewhere in the midst of my grief is the confidence that spring will come.

When you find yourself overpowered by melancholy, the best way is to go out and do something kind to somebody.

—JOHN KEBLE

When our grief is fresh and acute, our own suffering probably *is* all we can attend to.

But melancholy is often a long-term thing, a kind of low-key sadness. It is almost worse than fresh grief because its onset is back there somewhere—we can hardly remember when we didn't feel this way. And furthermore, we see no end in sight.

If we are feeling serious depression, we're more likely to go for help. But melancholy? Well, maybe we can pull ourselves out of it. It's worth a try. And one of the best attempts is to do something for someone else—a phone call to a lonely person, some flowers or homemade bread to a shut-in, an offer to read in the library's program for the visually impaired. It will take us out of ourselves for a bit. And the interaction with another will restore some of our fallen energy.

I'll be on the lookout for something I can do for others when melancholy closes in around me.

APRIL 30

Oh, if I had Orpheus' voice and poetry
with which to move the Dark Maid and her Lord,
I'd call you back, dear love, from the world below.
I'd go down there for you. Charon or the grim
King's dog could not prevent me then
from carrying you up into the fields of light.

—EURIPIDES

It is a longing we have—to be able to recover the lost, to bring our dear loves back to life. It is a fantasy, a myth, as old as there are recorded tales. If only we had the right words . . . if only we could get past the guardians of the dead . . .

Perhaps these longings, these fantasies, are our way of getting used to the idea, by trial and error, that this separation will last as long as our own life lasts.

Not that there won't be ways our life will continue to be blessed, to be fed, by the memory and spirit of our loved one, but in terms of physical presence in this life—it is over.

But perhaps these fantasies also help us keep alive the hope that on the other side of death we will be reunited—that there is a place where our loved one is indeed present, and waits for us.

Could this recurring image of my search for you support a faith that I may one day find you?

Believe that life is worth living and your belief will help create the fact.

—WILLIAM JAMES

At first we are so overwhelmed by loss that we seem powerless to do anything more than ride along on the turbulent sea of our sorrow and distress. There is no use in trying to steer this craft. It's enough just to stay afloat.

But after a while we begin to get some sense that we do, in fact, have some choice about which way to go.

This is often an unwelcome discovery. It is easier to drift, and people are so sympathetic to our situation when we are sad. It is comforting—and less work—to continue to bathe in that sympathy.

But our life is at a standstill, and we don't want that to last forever.

Now we have choices to make, and choice involves risk. One of the risks open to us is to act from the assumption that life is, in fact, worth living, and that we can help ourselves to confirm it. How? The whole theory of behavior modification is that if we change our behavior, our attitudes will also change. We can begin to *do* things again. We can make an effort to smile. We can reach out to someone else in need.

I will try acting as though life is worth living, and see what happens!

MAY 2

Anyone who tells a story speaks a world into being.
—MICHAEL WILLIAMS

One of the customs we have seen develop at memorial services is to have friends and loved ones share stories about the one who has died—tender moments, jokes, and anecdotes of their life together. These bring their own joy and serve to lighten the sadness of loss.

We have done the same thing in a less formal setting when after the services are over, family and friends gather for refreshment and find themselves lapsing into fond reminiscence—stories from recent times or from long ago.

I recall returning home from the cemetery after my father's death and how family and friends assembled to share food and conversation. After a while someone said, "Wouldn't George have enjoyed this party!" and someone else said, "Perhaps he's enjoying it now." Surely all of us felt his spirit among us.

Especially if death has come under particularly hard circumstances, as in the death of a child, friends may think it an act of kindness to refrain from mentioning the child. All the more reason to "speak into being" a life that has ended so soon. Because a life is over doesn't mean that that life won't continue to enrich and bless the living.

Shared stories are a gift to the teller and to the one who hears.

It is unwise, because it is untrue, to idealize the dead . . . We will spend a lot of needed energy keeping that illusion in place and we will not honor the vigor and truth of the [one] who has died . . . The myth of perfection is hard to maintain. We do not need it. We can give it over—to God, if you will. Lay it down. Leave it there. The [person], as he or she was, was God's child, acceptable, loved, all right. And so are we.

—MARTHA WHITMORE HICKMAN

This impulse to idealize the dead may spring from the sobering realization that for our loved one, any possibility for further human interaction or enhancement of reputation is gone.

Perhaps the impulse to idealize a loved one—and our relationship to that loved one—comes from our own anxiety about a relationship that had its ups and downs, and now the chances for fixing that are over.

Of course our loved one had some weaknesses. Of course our relationship had its ups and downs. Join the human race! What is not helpful is some fretful—and wasted—effort to maintain a rosy gloss over the human triumphs and shortcomings which are part of each and every life.

To berate myself or my loved one over what is unfixable only deepens the wounds. In love and trust I can acknowledge who we were and are to each other, and then move on.

May 4

Look upon each day that comes as a challenge, as a test of courage. The pain will come in waves, some days worse than others, for no apparent reason. Accept the pain. Do not suppress it. Never attempt to hide grief from yourself. Little by little, just as the deaf, the blind, the handicapped develop with time an extra sense to balance disability, so the bereaved, the widowed, will find new strength, new vision, born of the very pain and loneliness which seem, at first, impossible to master.

—DAPHNE DU MAURIER

When the waves of pain rise highest, we think we will be swept under, that we cannot make it. But we can. Our work then is to accept the pain, and to wait. We can do other things while waiting—talk with people, go to the store, read, work in the garden. Even as we do these things we are aware of the pain, scraping against our heart. But if we accept these bad days as part of the course of healing, then better days, better moods, will come. The pain will moderate, and we can be confident—proud, even—in our newly acquired strength.

I will not try to hide or walk around it. I will walk through the center of my sorrow and I will emerge—proud and strong.

When you pass through the waters I will be with you:
    and through the rivers, they shall not overwhelm you;
when you walk through fire you shall not be burned,
    and the flame shall not consume you.

—ISAIAH 43:2

We are never promised freedom from flood and fire, from any kind of disaster, or freedom from death.

What God is promising here is that we do not walk through these terrors alone and that, difficult as they are, they will not destroy us.

But we have to act to take advantage of this promise.

Can we reach out our hand into the darkness, believing there is One there to sustain us, to help us through this terrible time? There is a saying that for every halting step we take toward God, God walks a thousand miles in blazing light to come to us.

I will reach out my hand into the darkness, trusting that I do not go alone.

MAY 6

The warm air makes me dream of what was, and of what would be if you were here. I know that this dream is but an inaptitude to live the present. I allow myself to drift on this current without looking too far or too deep. I await the moment when I will find my strength again. It will come.

—ANNE PHILIPE

Our world is full of things that will take us back into the past, remind us of our loved one and what we have lost by his or her passing. Old songs. Fragrances. Seasonal changes of weather. Holidays. Birthdays. The list goes on.

Well, let them come, these reminders. Sometimes they bear with them a poignant sweetness. Sometimes we think they will break our hearts, so devastating is our sense of loss, brought into sharp focus again.

As time passes, these sieges will be more short-lived, easier to move through and come out on the other side.

It is well not to fight these images of a lost world, to let them pass through us—savoring their sweetness if it is there, bearing the pain while it lasts—knowing that in a little while we can lay claim to ourselves again.

The journeys into the past always include a way back into the present, which is where I live.

Never forget that you are not alone. The Divine is with you, helping and guiding. He is the companion who never fails, the friend whose love comforts and strengthens. Have faith and He will do everything for you.

—AUROBINDO (HINDU)

Loneliness is one of the afflictions of grief. We miss the one who has died, but that's not all. We miss the world the way it used to be, without this loss that shadows our every step. We miss our image of the future with this loved one in it.

We feel alone because so much of our life right now is internal—the agonizing questions, the turmoil. Who can share that with us? We feel separated from the rest of the world. We walk along the street and the people we pass seem carefree and unburdened. Of course that isn't so, but when our grief is so consuming, other people seem to be from an alien land.

Of course our families and friends are close, but even they cannot know the depths of our grief.

To whom to turn? It will help immeasurably if we can think of the Divine Presence, alive in us and in all of creation. A presence that stabilizes us, compassionately holds us, rides on our breath, brings us peace. Try it. Close your eyes and become familiar with this presence within you!

There is within me a Holy Presence—trustworthy, kind, strong.

MAY 8

I pray to the birds because I believe they will carry the messages of my heart upward. I pray to them because I believe in their existence, the way their songs begin and end each day—the invocations and benedictions of Earth. I pray to the birds because they remind me of what I love rather than what I fear. And at the end of my prayers, they teach me how to listen.

—TERRY TEMPEST WILLIAMS

Which of us has not felt his or her heart soar at the sight of birds flying across the sky? What a lift it gives us—their freedom, the formations they make as they turn and dip and then wheel off to some far place. They are a good way to symbolize the swirling currents of our life, the mysteries of beginnings and endings.

I remember visiting a friend's farm soon after my daughter's death. This friend had a swing hung from a tree limb. I got on the swing and pushed and pumped and, at the top of the arc, wondered what it would be like if I could just let go and fly up into the sky. I think it was one of my first occasions of hope—that I could make it through, that brighter days were coming.

In a world of such beauty as birds in flight, surely I can come to feel at home again, even after my loss. And if, in thought, I attach myself to birds in flight, who knows where that may take me?

Were it possible for us to see further than our knowledge reaches, and yet a little way beyond the outworks of our divining, perhaps we would endure our sadnesses with greater confidence than our joys. For they are the moments when something new has entered into us, something unknown; our feelings grow mute in shy perplexity, everything in us withdraws, a stillness comes, and the new, which no one knows, stands in the midst of it and is silent.

—MARIA RAINER RILKE

These times of grieving the loss of a loved one are times of change. It is as though we leave forever a room where we have been comfortable and functioning well, and enter a new room. Some of the same furnishings are there, and some of the same people, but the room is different nonetheless and requires a whole new adaptation from us—and, probably, from the others in the room with us.

We have choices. We can hide in a corner, cowering, unwilling to look around. We can tear around mindlessly, looking for an escape, though we know there is none. Or we can look around, see where the windows are and where doors open into the future, for the door we came through is closed. We can look for people who can help us—and begin to attend to this life, day by day.

Slowly, and with some ambivalence, I will begin to experience the new in my life.

MAY 10

Each substance of a grief hath twenty shadows.
—WILLIAM SHAKESPEARE

They are everywhere—the reminders of our loss. They ricochet off one another, fill the empty spaces of our lives.

My granddaughter comes to visit. She is just the age—two and a half—my daughter was when she was flower girl in my sister's wedding. I have saved the dress. It fits my dark-haired granddaughter as it fit my dark-haired daughter. My granddaughter tries it on, turns this way and that in front of the mirror. "I like it," she says. It is hers.

My daughter lived more than a dozen years after she wore that dress. And yet . . . the dress calls back not only the delight we all took in that wedding, but the death years later of the one who wore the dress.

Later in the visit, I read to this small, wonderful child a story that had been a favorite of my daughter's. Behind my voice I hear my daughter's voice at two and a half, anticipating the words as we turned each page. The reminder is a shadow. It is also sunlight—wonderful, life-giving sunlight—that this precious child whom my daughter never saw delights in her dress and in her storybook, and that I am a bridge between these two.

There is no shadow without sunlight behind it.

Out of every crisis comes the chance to be reborn, to reconceive ourselves as individuals, to choose the kind of change that will help us to grow and to fulfill ourselves more completely.

—NENA O'NEILL

We know that one does not come through a grief unscathed. What we sometimes don't fully recognize is the power we have, after the first grief has passed, to choose what we are going to make of ourselves, bereft though we are.

In a way, we resist claiming this power. We are tired. We don't want to be held responsible. We are hurt. We want to be taken care of, tenderly, not to be told we have to forge a new beginning.

We all know of people who, after a devastating loss, go on to reshape their lives in heroic terms. I think of Elizabeth Gray Vining, whose husband died when they were both very young, and who went on to become tutor to the Crown Prince of Japan.

We have choices to make and, as survivors of crisis, we have new strength, new power—if we chose to claim them.

"When life hands you a lemon, make lemonade."

May 12

Her love is everywhere. It follows me as I go about the house, meets me in the garden, sends swans into my dreams. In a strange, underwater or above earth way I am very nearly happy.

—Sylvia Townsend Warner

In a strange, paradoxical way, the dead do seem to accompany us, like a shadow only slightly removed from our own being. I don't think this happens in any sustained fashion right away. Perhaps we have to wait a while, know the reality of separation, and give ourselves time for the components of our lives to sift down into their new patterns before we can begin to see that the relationship with the one who has died is not over. It is different, but it is not over. It is not what we would wish, but it has its own reality and comfort.

Perhaps our sense of the loved one comes unbidden; perhaps we invoke it by our thoughts. It comes to us in different ways—a sense of the person's presence, of warmth and love in the room. A dream that speaks directly to our need.

Long ago, when my grief was still quite new, I wondered aloud to my son about the origin and meaning of one of these experiences—Was it real? Could I trust it? And he said, "Why don't you just accept it as a gift?"

I will listen. I will welcome as gifts the memory and presence of love.

Go in all simplicity; do not be anxious to win a quiet mind, and it will be all the quieter. Do not examine so closely into the progress of your soul. Do not crave so much to be perfect, but let your spiritual life be formed by your duties, and by the actions which are called forth by circumstances. Do not take overmuch thought for tomorrow. God, who has led you safely on so far, will lead you on to the end.

—FRANCIS DE SALES

So much goes churning through our mind when we are recovering from grief: our memories of our loved one, the circumstances of death, how we felt and behaved at the time of death and in the ensuing days. We want to be "good grievers"—which may mean giving full expression to our grief so it won't stay there undigested in our hearts. Other times a kind of numbness takes over, and we wonder about that—*What's the matter with me that I can't cry?*

This taking of our emotional temperature can be exhausting. If we feel we are being too introspective, we can try to shut that off for a while—go for a walk, watch some lightweight television show, do something that requires mental concentration so we don't assess how our spirits are, moment by moment.

I'm doing fine, just the way I am. Now I'll forget about it for a while.

MAY 14

The chessboard is the world; the pieces are the phenomena of the universe; the rules of the game are what we call the Laws of Nature. The player on the other side is hidden from us. We know that his play is always fair, just and patient.

—THOMAS HUXLEY

If we could stand back far enough to see, as astronauts do, the whirling globe, the swirls of blue and green, would we be better able to cope with our catastrophes?

If our view were long-range enough so we could watch ourselves from astronomic space or geologic time, would we not see how it all fits together—the living and those who have gone through the gateway of death all part of the same creation? And all of us building, forming, watching, empowered by the Light Invisible. We who have stood at the doorway of death, watching our loved one pass through, are entitled to all flights of imagination as we contemplate the unknown.

I can step from the bonds of The Known and let my spirit soar.

This we owe our beloved dead, whether young or old: to wipe from our memories all that was less than their best, and to carry them in our hearts at their wisest, most compassionate, most creative moments. Is that not what all of us hope from those who survive us?
—ELIZABETH WATSON

In the end we owe them this—and probably give it gladly—and hope for it for ourselves. But let's not be too quick to remake the image of the dead. We need to remember our loved ones in their totality, or we will end up with shadow memories, endowed only with half light. Surely our memories of our loved ones are wide enough to encompass all of their natures, including the shortcomings and errors which are the human lot. The foibles of our loved ones can provide food for laughter, anger, tears—the stuff of family bonding.

Then, as all these memories sift through the screens of time and the basic love in which we hold one another, what will stay in our minds will be the most endearing and wisest qualities, with enough fragments of foible and shortcoming, remembered in forgiveness and love, to make us human.

◆◆

In the remembered image of a loved one there is room—and affection—for the person in his or her fullness.

MAY 16

. . . even dead her familiar face made him safe . . . as if she actually told him, "I died, that's all."

Tears came, and that was it. He held her hand.

It was then for the first time I saw them as they really were. She, who I once knew as the beginning and end of everything warm and soft, my only real absolution for everything, was just a girl, in a blouse with a lace collar, whose name he couldn't guess, and he was a handsome boy with blonde hair, and they met at Coney Island one afternoon.

—JOSEPH PINTAURO

When our loved ones leave us, one of the ways we keep their presence alive is by retelling the stories. How was it when they were younger? What were their favorite stories about themselves? About us?

Now that they are gone, our imaginations are somehow freed to claim them in a more expanded way—fanciful and yet true. Our nostalgia is genuine. It is also benevolent and tender. We see them in their fragility, as figures in a drama suspended in time, taking their places along with the legendary figures they used to tell us about. Perhaps we know them in greater clarity—and charity—than we could when we were engaged in the dynamics of daily exchange.

My life will continue to be blessed as the stories of my loved one develop and settle in my mind.

I will miss seeing her face and hearing her voice and knowing she was always there close to me. She has crossed a river from me that I must wait to cross before I see her again. When I see a river, I will think of her.

—TERRY KAY

How we miss the common everyday companionship of our loved one—the face across the table, the presence in bed, the voice calling our name.

There is a way in which this presence lingers for a long time, until the wound heals enough that we are able, finally, to acknowledge the separation.

Then our image of our loved one can become more focused, rather than scattered here and there in all the places we were used to their being. They have indeed "crossed a river."

It is helpful to play through this fantasy in our head. The image is strong, and fitting, as evidenced by its use in myths about the passage into death. I remember doing just this with the help of a therapist friend—in my mind coming to a river and relinquishing my daughter's hand and watching her cross over. I remember the struggle, and the tears, and, finally, the sense of relief—that the truth had been honored, that she was safe, that I would cross the same river when my time came.

◆◆

When I see a river, I will think of you.

MAY 18

The world is not divided into the strong who care and the weak who are cared for. We must each in turn care and be cared for, not just because it is good for us, but because it is the way things are.

—Sheila Cassidy

Sometimes we who are struggling with grief have a hard time acknowledging our need to be cared for. Are we being weak? Are we drawing attention to ourselves? Particularly if we are used to being "helpers," we are sometimes not comfortable in the role of the person who needs help. Perhaps we are too proud to let others see we are in pain. Besides, in view of all the pain and suffering in the world—nations facing starvation, whole segments of society living under terrible conditions—how can we ask for a part of the world's care for our own private grief?

Goodness knows there is more than enough grief in the world to go around. But life is lived one human being at a time, and while we do what we can to ease the burdens of others, there are times when our own burdens are heavy, and we need help. For a time we may need more than what we see as our "share" of help. Never mind. It is our need. It is our turn. We are entitled.

I am a human being and I don't need to put up a facade of strength.

She thought of the women at Chicken Little's funeral . . .
What she had regarded since as unbecoming behavior
seemed fitting to her now; they were screaming at the
neck of God, his giant nape, the vast back-of-the-head
that he had turned on them in death. But it seemed to her
now it was not a fist-shaking grief they were keening but
rather a simple obligation to say something, do something, feel something about the dead. They could not let
that heart-smashing event pass unrecorded, unidentified.
—TONI MORRISON

Many of us have been slow to recognize the value of expressing the full force of anguish and despair. We may
think displays of strong emotions are somehow unseemly.

Grief is not a test. There's no grading. No passing or
failing. But if our tendency is to clamp down on our feelings because we think it's better for us or less disturbing
to others, we might try going somewhere we're not likely
to be heard—and let it out. Scream. Yell. Berate. Wail.
Pound on the wall.

Some hospitals have "screaming rooms"—places where
the newly bereaved can go and scream and rail without
fear of disturbing others and/or embarrassing themselves.

Not a pretty sight or sound? A human sound.

I will take my cues from within, and not be afraid.

MAY 20

So often, we believe that we have come to a place that is void of hope and void of possibilities, only to find that it is the very hopelessness that allows us to hit bottom, give up our illusion of control, turn it over, and ask for help. Out of the ashes of our hopelessness comes the fire of our hope.

—ANNE WILSON SCHAEF

When one is low enough, bottoming out on despair and hopelessness, the thought of going anywhere at all is totally foreign. It's not that it would be too hard, it's simply that the prospect of any motion is unthinkable. Like a mule that refuses to budge, life seems to have stopped in its tracks—and no flattery, no promises, no cajoling, no threats, can have any effect. The future has no appeal and no promise.

At this point the path of integrity and, ultimately, of a return to health may be found by standing still and acknowledging the degree to which one's life is filled to the edges with grief. But after a while even the grieving heart becomes restless and thinks, This will not do forever. One begins to look around, maybe step out of the picture, as it were, leave that darkness behind, and begin to walk away, noticing a flower growing along the path, a waft of cloud in a blue sky, a friend who has been waiting all along.

At the bottom of the well, one can look up and see the sky.

Let it not be death but completeness.
Let love melt into memory and pain into songs.
Let the flight through the sky end in the folding of the
   wings over the nest.
Let the last touch of your hands be gentle like the flower
   of the night.
Stand still, O Beautiful End, for a moment, and say your
   last words in silence.
I bow to you and hold up my lamp to light you on your
   way.

—RABINDRANATH TAGORE

So can we ease our loved ones into the land beyond, wishing for them a safe and gentle passage. In a holy silence we hold a lamp to guide them on their way.

It is a leap of faith to trust that all is well, even harder to fantasize holding a lamp to guide them, since we probably are not ready to have them go.

But the choice is not ours, whether they go or stay. Our choice is how we respond to their going, how we think about it.

If we can think about it in the lyrical imagery of Tagore, maybe that in itself will ease our pain.

I cannot know where you are going, but I hold the lamp of my love aloft to accompany you on your way.

MAY 22

Tonight all the hells of young grief have opened up again; the mad words, the bitter resentment, the fluttering in the stomach, the nightmare reality, the wallowed-in tears. For in grief nothing "stays put." One keeps on emerging from a phase, but it always recurs. Round and round. Everything repeats. Am I going in circles, or dare I hope I am on a spiral?

—C. S. Lewis

It comes without warning, the feeling of being plunged back into the freshness of new grief—the same bewilderment, the feeling of being disoriented, our life disorganized. Often we don't know just what has set us off again. And we thought we were doing better!

The loved one we have lost has probably been with us for a very long time, perhaps all of our life—as when a parent has died. It is going to take us a long time to adapt to that loss. It won't happen smoothly, either, in some sort of gradual uphill climb out of the valley of despair. It's more like the work of clearing a rock-strewn New England field. With great labor the rocks are removed, but then the land shifts, the seasons change, and new rocks work their way to the surface. Eventually the land will be cleared, but it may take a long time!

I will be gentle with myself, accepting these storms of the psyche as part of my passage on the road to recovery.

All goes onward and outward, nothing collapses,
And to die is different from what any one supposes, and
luckier.

—WALT WHITMAN

Can we read in the flow of life, in the return of songbirds
and roses and blueberries, some reassurance that it is life's
intention to waste nothing, but to keep the basic substance
of life itself going? And if this is true for the smaller, less
complex works of creation, surely it must be true for the
intricate and wondrous creation which is a human being.

Death helps to define our life, to give it some framework
and the urge to do and be what we can because an end to
life as we know it will come.

And then what? None of us knows. But we can take
some clues from what we do know of the rest of creation.
The clues lead us to hope, as do the stories of dying persons whose faces become suffused with joy and wonder.
Not all dying persons have such an experience. We don't
need a hundred percent validation, any more than we
need to add up all the columns of figures in the world to
know that two plus two equals four—every time.

When facing the unknown, hope is as reasonable as despair.

MAY 24

The moment comes when our eyes are opened, and we see and realize that grace is infinite. Grace, my friends, demands nothing from us but that we shall await it with confidence and acknowledge it in gratitude . . . that which we have chosen is given us, and that which we have refused is also, and at the same time, granted us . . . that which we have rejected is poured upon us abundantly.

—ISAK DINESEN

All the lost hopes, all the lost plans for the future when a loved one dies . . . how are we to accept these losses?

In Dinesen's story "Babette's Feast" General Lowenhielm returns to the scene of a brief and unconsummated love and makes the astonishing statement that the years of deprivation are redeemed by the grace of this moment.

Can we expect such a moment of grace? What might it be?

Perhaps in some solitary moment we sense the almost palpable presence of our loved one in the room, participating with us in some of the ventures of our life.

Perhaps on some family occasion when we would have expected only yearning grief, we have in addition to the sadness a sense of the loved one taking it in, smiling, blessing the occasion.

Or perhaps we experience a surge of confident hope that we shall, on some other plane, be together again.

In the midst of absence, a presence is made known.

There is no question of getting beyond it. The little boat enters the dark fearful gulf and our only cry is to escape—"put me on land again." But it's useless. Nobody listens. The shadowy figure rows on. One ought to sit still and uncover one's eyes.

—KATHERINE MANSFIELD

Perhaps we try to escape.

If we do not speak of it . . .

If we drink ourselves into numbness . . .

If we submerge ourselves in work so we don't have time to dwell on it . . .

If we sleep, we will forget . . .

But our silence shouts to us. Drugs will destroy us. At the end of the harried workday we look in the mirror and see our despair. And when we escape into sleep—we have to face the truth all over again when we wake up.

Years ago I was riding on a ferris wheel with my daughter and, being fearful of heights and imagining all kinds of accidents, I covered my eyes with my hands.

She would have none of it. "Open your eyes, Mom!" she called.

I did, and it wasn't so scary after all.

Better to open our eyes and face our loss. It will cost less in the long run.

MAY 26

The refusal to love is the only unbearable thing.
—MADELEINE L'ENGLE

Sometimes it seems that this grief we are experiencing is the only unbearable thing.

But think—if we had no one we loved enough to mourn for, how flat, how terrible, our lives would be.

And this particular person . . . what would our life have been without this one whom we loved so much? Was it worth the pain we are experiencing to have had this loved one for the time that we did?

Yes, but—

Of course. This grief is not to be dismissed by some attempted appeal to reason. Not now. Not ever. But it may help from time to time to look on the underside of this pain—as one lifts a leaf to look at the silvery underside—and note what riches we have had in the life of this one whose death we mourn.

Sometime down the road—and when that will be is as variable as the people who mourn—the grief will be on the underside and the sense of blessing and gratitude will be the bright surface, luminous and green.

Sometimes when the pain is overwhelming, I will try to surround myself with the memory of love.

I wouldn't mind dying young . . . I've had a full life already.

—MARY HICKMAN

We who have lost loved ones through sudden accidents find ourselves scouring our memories for portents. Were there any clues, any indicators, that something terrible like this might happen? If we can find them, perhaps they inject a measure of meaning into a life thrown into chaos. On some subconscious level did our loved one know?

My daughter made that statement, casually, during the months preceding her sudden death at sixteen in a horseback-riding accident. "Mary!" I said. "One world at a time."

After she died I remembered her words. Had she known better than I? And what is going on, that it may be possible to have some vague foreknowledge of an event like that?

If that is possible, what other unfathomable mysteries exist in a universe of which we may know only the smallest fragment?

These "signs and wonders" do not mitigate the sorrow of loss, but they may give us hope that on some level a Transcendant Scheme is at work and knows what it's doing.

I will keep my mind open to all possibilities of knowledge and faith.

MAY 28

O God, you have let me pass the day in peace;
let me pass the night in peace, O Lord who has no lord.
There is no strength but in you. You alone have no
  obligation.
Under your hand I pass the night. You are my Mother
  and my Father. Amen.
                        —TRADITIONAL BORAN (AFRICAN) PRAYER

To have passed any length of time in peace when we are
grieving is an achievement. It is not to be counted on: we
do well to invoke help for another stretch of peace. And
to invoke help from one who is totally available.

It is a touching piece of wisdom in this prayer that the
one who prays, prays to a Lord who doesn't have prior
commitments—*Pay attention to me, please.*

The appeal is to our ultimate experience of comfort and
safety—a mother and a father. And yet—a gentle reminder—not a distracted mother and father, please, but
one who can pay full attention. Then we can afford to trust
that mother and father to see us through the night.

In my weakness I can turn in trust to One who is strong.

Did someone say that there would be an end,
An end, Oh, an end, to love and mourning?
                                        —MAY SARTON

No, not to either. And that's the comfort, I suppose—that though we don't ever "get over" a major loss, we don't "get over" the love we shared with that person, either—a love that, in ways we will come to know, stays with us and continues to enrich our life over the years.

But, a caution. We need not confuse the mourning with the image of the person we loved. If we allow them to overlap too much, then we cannot let go of the mourning because we would lose the loved one, too. But they are different, and we will do better with our lives if, as soon as we are able, we make a conscious separation of the loved person from the grief over his or her loss. Each has its place, but they don't always need to blend together.

◆◆

Though I know my memory of my loved one will always carry a tinge of sadness, I will be able to put that in the background—if I want to.

MAY 30

Grief melts away
Like snow in May,
As if there were no such cold thing.

—GEORGE HERBERT

We thought it would never happen—that this grief would never ease, let alone melt away.

Yet grief, like the snow, does melt slowly away, until one day, perhaps to our surprise, we realize the landscape has changed—the snow has gone. Grass and stone and flower beds are visible again. Similarly, our grief seeps slowly away, until one day we realize we are feeling better—almost like ourselves again.

To extend the metaphor—the melting snow, which became water, has gone on to nourish this or other ground, depending on how the land lies and where the earth is thirstiest. Or perhaps the moisture is caught up in the clouds, to drift over the sky and then to descend again to water other lands.

In the same way our grief becomes transmuted into other forms of energy and life. It will continue to be part of the system of our life and the lives of those around us, depending on circumstances and where the need is greatest. It will not be lost. It will be transformed.

I will entrust to the processes of life this grief which lies so cold against my heart.

There is not one life which the Life-giver ever loses out of His sight; not one which sins so that He casts it away; not one which is not so near to Him that whatever touches it touches Him with sorrow or with joy.

—PHILLIPS BROOKS

Particularly if we have been care-givers for the one who has died, it is hard to be free of the irrational question, "Who is taking care of him or her now?" Who we wonder, is befriending our loved one? Who is standing close by to comfort and assure, to show a newcomer to The Other Side what to do, how it all works?

These questions are especially persistent and troubling if the one who has died is a child or a young person—someone who has needed our care, someone who's likely to feel insecure in new situations.

On one level these are irrational, needless questions. But death is often not rational at all, and certainly the questions that swirl around the subject trigger our most primordial and elusive anxieties and hopes.

We grope for images to calm our fears. Phillips Brooks's figure of the Life-giver rings true—and is just what we need!

Into your hands—You, ever-present, ever-caring power of life and love—I commend my loved one.

JUNE 1

We must be ready to allow ourselves to be interrupted by God.

—DIETRICH BONHOEFFER

Who is ready? We have our plans, things we're looking forward to—life going on at its sometimes unpleasant but nontheless predictable pace.

Then something happens—like an accident, or a death, or an illness—that changes everything, forces us to reappraise our priorities and, often, reset our lives.

People who have come close to disaster and been able to wheel free have shown a renewed appreciation for the simple pleasures of life, for the gift of each day, and a resolve not to put off pleasures or acts of kindness until "another day," because "another day" may not come.

We who have lost loved ones have also learned the value of simple gifts, of not putting off kind words or actions, because we never know when events will change our world, the expected developments of our lives, and the intended recipients of our kind words and actions may be gone.

The preciousness of this day is its own gift.

Our joys as winged dreams do fly;
Why then should sorrow last?
Since grief but aggravates thy loss,
Grieve not for what is past.

—THOMAS PERCY

Does grief aggravate our loss?

There is a delicate balance at stake here.

On the one hand, we need to pay attention to grief, to grieve our way through the valley of loss, or we will never be able to assimilate the loss, to be whole people again. On the other hand, we need not linger overlong on the way, or we may get stuck and never come through.

If we find ourselves repeatedly dwelling for a long time on how bad we feel, we might try instead to dwell on some of the joys that fly "as winged dreams"—wonderful times we have shared with our loved one. Or times that have nothing to do with him or her but have brought us joy.

We do have some control over how long we let our attention linger. So let's not allow the joyous subjects to get away too soon. We need them!

From time to time I will step into my rooms of joyous memories—and close the doors!

JUNE 3

How soon unaccountable I became tired and sick,
Till rising and gliding out I wander'd off by myself,
In the mystical moist night air, and from time to time,
Look'd up in perfect silence at the stars.

—WALT WHITMAN

How readily we can identify with Whitman's restlessness.

Sometimes it seems as though nothing can hold our attention, nothing is worth doing for long. Life seems flat, without sparkle, almost without meaning.

Then how reassuring it can be to go out into the quiet night and look up at the stars. Surely in a world of such vast beauty and order, such unfathomable reaches of time and space, there must be meanings beyond our understanding.

There is a sense of intimacy to the night, too. That nearest star, bright in the heavens—is it a sign?

The mystery remains. But somehow we are comforted.

Even in my loneliness and sorrow, the world holds me in its embrace.

Truly, it is allowed to weep. By weeping, we disperse our wrath; and tears go through the heart, even like a stream.

—OVID

We know this by our experience. We speak of having "a good cry." Or someone says, "I felt better once I could cry." Usually we do feel better, though if we have succumbed to tears in a public place, we may feel a little abashed.

Why? I have never seen anyone turn away in impatience or disgust from someone who was crying genuine tears. If I had I would more readily think of the observer as disturbed than the one who wept.

To release the pressure of grief (including, as Ovid describes, the "wrath" of grief) feels almost like a phenomenon of physics—a matter of releasing internal pressure. It has also been suggested that tears are good chemistry—they wash undesirable elements out of our system.

There are people who, because of illness or emotional constraint, are not able to cry. How sad that is.

So let the tears flow. If your eyes get red and your cheeks get puffy, who cares? Your face will soon return to normal and you'll feel a whole lot better in the meantime.

I am grateful for the gift of being able to cry.

JUNE 5

Lying awake at dawn, I remember them,
With a love that is almost joy I remember them:
Lost, and all mine, all mine, forever.
—JOHN HALL WHEELOCK

It is a bittersweet joy, but real nonetheless—the way our lost loves are forever in our hearts and minds. They are, in fact, constant to our consciousness in a way they couldn't be when they were alive, because then we depended on their comings and goings—the highs and lows of their being with us, the vagaries of presence and convenience.

But now we can summon the memories of them at will, and even when we're not consciously thinking of them, they seem almost as integral to our being as our skin, or as a comfortable robe we wrap ourselves in at the end of a busy and tiring day. A loved one—a memory to be with, a quiet companion.

It is, again, not what we would have chosen. But it is its own blessing.

I will relax into the memory and spiritual presence of my loved one, and feel at peace.

Learning to trust will be for all of us the means by which the root system grows firm and nourishes the tree of life.
—ELAINE M. PREVALLET

All winter, in many parts of the country, the earth has lain brown and barren—or covered with chilling snow.

But beneath that apparently lifeless earth the roots of plants have maintained themselves in a necessary hibernation. Then, come spring, year after year (with a little help from us!), the earth comes to life again, and blooms with beauty and nurturance.

Maybe this can be a model of trust for us in these new-green months of early summer—that the season of depression and sorrow will, in time, give way to a renewed love of life and appreciation for its gifts—including the gift of the life and the legacy of the one we have loved.

As I have learned to trust the turning of the seasons, may I trust the life that supports me in my journey through grief.

JUNE 7

We cannot re-create this world . . . We cannot even, truly, re-create ourselves. Only our behavior can we re-create, or create anew.

—ALICE WALKER

How can we move ourselves out of the valley of despondency into which grief is apt to plunge us?

Not by changing the fact of loss. We know better than to hope for that. Not by some sweeping act of will that shifts our spirit from sadness into acceptance and an eagerness to live again. We may have tried that, but it doesn't work: at best, we achieve a momentary change of heart, but it will not last.

There is a classic line of thought in Christian spirituality that says the way to test the validity of the faith is to act as though it is true, and see what happens.

In the same way, we can begin to act as though we have an investment in the future, as though we are rejoining our life's activities, and reenjoying our life—our friends, our gardens, our music, our work—and see what happens.

I will step back into the stream of life—and see what happens.

Then let not winter's ragged hand deface
In thee thy summer, ere thou be distilled.
—WILLIAM SHAKESPEARE

Grief hangs on and on, and some days we think we will never come out from under its shadow.

Sometimes we have no choice. It hits us like a physical blow, and it takes us a long time to get our breath back.

But sometimes we do have a choice. It's well to be reminded of that, though we may resist the notion, thinking—*There is no grief like this. How could I possibly move away from it?*

But perhaps we could. It's at least worth trying—to lay aside for a while the pall which has covered us since we lost our loved one.

Visualize lifting a heavy shroud from your head and shoulders, folding it carefully, tucking it away tenderly on a closet shelf, closing the door, and walking away.

Now (if no one's looking to wonder what on earth you're doing!) pantomime this action with your body. Go ahead—lift the heavy cloth, fold it, get up and walk to a closet and lay it on a shelf. Then close the door, lean against the door for a minute. And walk away.

And for a while, at least, savor the reality of this day, this summer day.

I do have some choice about when grief is primary in my life.

JUNE 9

> Above all, do not lose your desire to walk. Every day I walk myself into a state of well-being, and walk away from every illness. I have walked myself into my best thoughts, and I know of no thought so burdensome that one cannot walk away from it.
>
> —SÖREN KIERKEGAARD

I suppose it doesn't have to be walking, though walking is usually available and certainly one of the best ways to exercise. It is an empowering physical action that takes you somewhere—you're acting out the movement away from sadness and depression.

Sometimes it is hard for us to muster the energy to get up and go, but if we wait until we "feel like it," we may never get off the chair—or bed!

But it is hard to overestimate the value of walking. People whose emotional equilibrium is fragile are urged to walk. Part of the regimen for recovery from heart surgery is walking. A writer friend, when she gets to a rough place in her manuscript, will take what she refers to as her "thinking walk," and invariably comes back with new ideas.

So if we are having a hard time getting "unstuck" from spinning our wheels in regret or despair—try walking.

Nobody home—I've gone for a walk!

. . . he was catapulted into a whole new world, and lost in it. The sky was different. A ham sandwich was different. His own shoes lined up in the closet this morning had looked so unusual, he said, that he could hardly reach for them.

—JOSEPHINE HUMPHRIES

It is a continuing astonishment, running into the ordinary world we were used to. Now we see everything through a scrim of grief and loss. Of course the world looks different.

Would it be easier if we could be transported to some setting where we weren't always reminded of who is missing, who was here the last time we went to this particular store or drove along this particular country road?

Some people, with this very thought in mind, go away from home the first Christmas, or vacation somewhere other than the usual family spot. They won't have to endure the familiar setting with its constant reminder—a perpetual "What's wrong with this picture?"

Yet the usual patterns of our daily life are what, eventually, most of us will have to contend with, to build a new world within the world we know. And after a while we will find, to our surprise and contentment, that it feels like home again.

In the world I inhabit, I find steadiness, and a place to be.

JUNE 11

> But the souls of the righteous are in the hand of God, and there shall no torment touch them. In the sight of the unwise they seemed to die: and their departure is taken for misery, and their going from us to be utter destruction; but they are in peace.
>
> —THE WISDOM OF SOLOMON 3:1–3

These words from the ancient wisdom of the Apocrypha seem as contemporary now as they must have seemed when they were first written. Our anxiety, our perception, our hope, are all echoed here—as they have been through the writings of the ages.

It is comforting to see how constant have been the questions and answers about death and what lies beyond. If so many people, for so long, have strongly believed that when we die we return to God and are at peace, then surely we, too, can embrace this hope—for our loved ones, and for ourselves.

In the wisdom of the ages may I find solace and hope.

And then the idealization. Another distortion. Idealizing her in a way antithetical to her nature. Bella was no lofty madonna, no enigmatic Mary, no *mater dolorosa*. She was a flesh-and-blood lady who got her hands wet, whose life encompassed pain and suffering. A human being with human flaws. It's a betrayal to remember only the good parts,

—TOBY TALBOT

Not only is it a betrayal. It takes a lot of energy to maintain these faulty illusions—energy we need to attend to the rest of our grieving and the rest of our lives.

We may think we are honoring the dead by exaggerating their good qualities and dismissing what was less admirable. There is a precedent for this in the Latin admonition, *De mortuis nil nisi bonum.* Of the dead, nothing but good.

But it doesn't wash in the long run, if we are trying to remember in their fullness people we were close to and whom we loved.

What would we want for ourselves? To be remembered as some kind of paragon? Or to be remembered in full dimension as the people we are?

I celebrate the life of the one I loved—in all the fullness of his or her human qualities.

JUNE 13

I must learn to: open bottles, move the furniture, open stuck windows, go home alone, investigate the noise in the night, eat alone, make decisions alone, handle money alone, go on trips alone, fight with service companies alone, be sick alone, sleep alone, sing alone.

—SONJA O'SULLIVAN

Often we are better forewarned, better prepared, to deal with the big events like birthdays and holidays than with some of the more informal times when we have been accustomed to our loved one's presence. A woman whose husband had died said that the first time she heard some especially noteworthy news on the radio and turned around to relay the news to her husband—"That was when I knew he was gone."

Over time, the grooves of this new knowledge wear themselves into our brains, but it will take a while, and we will have many relapses—desperate yearnings for our loved ones to again fill their accustomed places.

But eventually the memory of their having shared this or that particular experience will carry a poignant gratitude for all the times they were with us. And we will find the power to go it alone.

As I learn my life anew, may I be empowered by loving memories.

God never says, you should have come yesterday;
   he never says, you must come again tomorrow,
but today if you will hear his voice,
   today he will hear you . . .
He brought light out of darkness,
   not out of lesser light;
he can bring thy summer out of winter,
   though thou have no spring.
All occasions invite his mercies,
   and all times are his seasons.

—JOHN DONNE

What do we think we must do, what must we believe, to feel any sense of ease from the pain of this grief?

There are no hoops to jump through, no concessions to a dogma we cannot believe. There are people who embody love for us. Can we believe that we are accepted, that there is in the universe a Oneness, an Embracing Love, a God—whatever word or impulse of mood seems possible to us? If we can, let us give over some of our grief to that Other, as in the dark a child hands over to a trusted friend some burden too heavy to carry.

No burden is too heavy—or too light.

No anxiety is too inconsequential—or too monumental.

May I not clutch my grief so tightly to myself that I cannot receive help when it is offered.

JUNE 15

We found that our circle of friends shifted . . . We were surprised and disappointed that people we thought were good friends became distant, uneasy, and seemed unable to help us. Others who were casual acquaintances became suddenly close, sustainers of life for us. Grief changes the rules, and sometimes rearranges the combinations.

—MARTHA WHITMORE HICKMAN

People often comment that those who feel most uneasy in speaking with us about our loss are protecting themselves from their own fear of loss and death.

There is nothing "right" or "wrong" about their attitude. They may not be aware of their own anxiety.

But it can be puzzling to us that people on whom we have relied in the past seem not as warmly supportive, as understanding, or as willing to be close as we would have expected. It's not their "fault." But it's important to recognize it's not *our* "fault," either. Circumstances change. Life deals us different experiences. So we may find ourselves drawn to former almost-strangers whose experiences echo our own.

On my life journey I will have many companions. I am grateful for my friends—old and new—and for the ways in which our stories draw us close.

I knew that . . . the full acceptance of the finality of loss, and all the pain that goes with it, need not diminish life but could give it a new quality of fulfillment. I also knew that this could not be achieved without going through the agonies of grief and mourning.

—LILY PINCUS

It is a brave statement, and for a while hard to believe, that going through a primary loss in one's life can lead to a greater sense of fulfillment. At first one thinks only of making it through the days and nights with any kind of equilibrium intact. The idea that there is a "bright side" to this is unbelievable, even offensive.

As with so many other major events in our lives, the wisdom comes only in retrospect, after we have had a chance to let the dust settle and see what we are left with. Then, indeed, we may recognize some wisdom we have won, some ability to bear pain and uncertainty.

But it doesn't come right away, and it can't be forced. And unless we let the various themes and demands of grief run their course, ask their questions, and honor their turmoil, we may never find a resolution at all.

I will not try to shortchange the process of grieving. I will take one day at a time.

JUNE 17

A new day rose upon me. It was as if another sun had risen in the sky; the heavens were indescribably brighter, and the earth fairer; and that day has gone on brightening to the present hour.

—ORVILLE DEWEY

When we are bogged down in heavy grief, can we believe such a day will ever come? A person recovering from a serious illness said, "It's almost worth having been sick, because I appreciate all over again how wonderful it is to be well."

It doesn't happen for a while. But if we are blessed with good friends and a faith that can help us through the bad times, then a time will come when we reawaken to the beauty of life around us as to a new June morning—to a world of incredible beauty and promise.

If you can't feel this way yet, stay with your grief. But keep the promise in mind that one day, having survived the worst, you will encounter the best, and probably with new appreciation because of what you have been through.

I will hold before myself the promise of a renewed and joyful life.

Nothing could stop you.
Not the best day. Not the quiet. Not the ocean rocking.
You went on with your dying.

—MARK STRAND

How they went on about their business, the dying. They knew we were there. They loved us, wished to spare us pain. Yes, they would miss us. But their eyes were already on another landscape, and we saw them pulling away.

Now that they are gone, do we feel abandoned?

No reason to. They love us still. They have reached a destination.

Do we need their permission to let them go? Surely they gave us that in dying.

Perhaps they need our permission to be fully at ease with their departure. A friend tells how, immediately after the death of a loved uncle, he felt the uncle's presence in the hall with him, and the question, "Is it all right to go, Buddy [the family's name for my friend]?" And he said, "Yes, it's all right," and felt the atmosphere change, a kind of peace and tranquility set in.

Death is a mystery in which the living are bystanders, but a mystery to be trusted.

JUNE 19

To have lived at all is a measure of immortality; for a baby to be born, to become a man, a woman, to beget others like himself, is an act of faith in itself, even an act of defiance. It is as though every human being born into this world burns, for a brief moment, like a star, and because of its pinpoint of light shines in the darkness, and so there is glory, so there is life.

—DAPHNE DU MAURIER

When we think of the processes of nature that brought about any one of us—the gene selection, the combination of that particular ovum and that particular sperm, our life in the womb, our transit into life as breathing, independent creatures—our being alive at all is in itself a miracle of survival and a cause for wonder and celebration. And so it is with the advent of our loved one upon the earth, and with the tides of kinship and love that cast us in the same scene, the same drama, together. Though we mourn the passing of that loved one, think how much poorer our lives would have been had we not inhabited the world together! While we hope for a continuation of life together beyond death, it is no small thing to have known and cherished one another in this spectacular setting—life.

I am grateful from the core of my being for the life I have shared with my loved one.

I am glad [the book] came to be written. It has in some strange way refined some dross out of me. It has taught me—though this was not my first lesson—to accept the joys and vicissitudes of life, and to fall in love again with its strangeness and beauty and terror.

—ALAN PATON

Not many of us will, like Alan Paton, write a book to help us work our way through loss. But many have found it helpful to keep a journal—a simple notebook in which to write our thoughts and questions, express our pain, so we don't have to carry it around in our heads all the time.

We may want to look back over the journal from time to time—to remind ourselves of the emotional ups and downs of our journey, or to refresh our minds about a sequence of events. If we never look at the pages again, they will still have served us well. Just finding words for the tumult helps us understand it a little better, move through it with less danger of getting stuck, so we can reach the place where we can "fall in love again" with life.

Of course, not everyone likes to write—painting does it for some, or playing the piano—anything to open our emotional pores and let the energy of grief flow out, free us for new life.

◆◆

Grief is like a refiner's fire. It will leave me with something beautiful.

JUNE 21

It isn't for the moment you are struck that you need courage, but for the long uphill climb back to sanity and faith and security.

—ANNE MORROW LINDBERGH

In the first flush of grief we are present to the needs of the occasion almost in spite of ourselves. The forms and customs of what to do next, how to behave, are pretty well prescribed, and we need muster only enough energy and will to follow along, do what is expected.

But then the rituals are over and life settles into a freer form. The decisions to be made are not about details of the service or where the visiting family members will sleep, but how to get on with our lives, what to do with the silences. Then we will need courage and fortitude.

And we will need these qualities for a long time as we struggle to regain our footing on a path that has drastically shifted. We will need courage for the daily walk, and confidence in the goals we have set—or reset—for ourselves now that one of our companions is no longer with us.

Give me courage for the long haul, and courage for each day's journey.

The present moment is significant, not as the bridge between past and future, but by reason of its contents, contents which can fill our emptiness and become ours, if we are capable of receiving them.

—DAG HAMMARSKJÖLD

When we are grieving, our minds are constantly flooded with memories from the past. Some memories call us back into that happier, more carefree world (or that's how we remember it!) before our lives were shaken by this loss. Other memories may be of times we regret, that now are impossible to "make up for." And when we are not remembering, we may be projecting into a future with its perpetually empty space—the years of missing our loved one.

But wait. *This* is the moment. This is the day we have.

As an exercise in receiving the contents of this day, try this. Stand where you are and imagine letting all the residue of the past, all thoughts about the future, slip away from you until they lie in a circle around your feet, like discarded clothes. Then step over them, walk into the next room, and look around.

◆◆

I will try to be fully present to this day—this day which is precious in itself and different from any other day I have had or will have.

JUNE 23

> . . .there is no more ridiculous custom than the one that makes you express sympathy once and for all on a given day to a person whose sorrow will endure as long as his life. Such grief, felt in such a way, is always "present," it is never too late to talk about it, never repetitious to mention it again.
>
> —MARCEL PROUST

This is a delicate point. Some people feel that to bring up an "old" grief is to reawaken a wound that has perhaps ceased to hurt—or at least to hurt as much.

Perhaps it depends on the severity of the loss. Where the loss seems lifelong and inappropriate—as in the death of a child—the grief is never "over." It will be at a different stage, but it is still there, and as parents, we may indeed be grateful that "after all this time" someone is mindful of a grief that, for us, never goes away.

I know that my husband and I were grateful on the several occasions when, a long time after our daughter's death, we encountered friends who had heard of our loss but had not seen us, and they took the occasion to express their sympathy. I expect that most of us would rather people risk offering too much than adopt some false constraint and leave us wondering whether they know or care.

Yes, I may cry when you speak of it, but I'm still glad for your support.

The sky is the daily bread of the eyes.
—RALPH WALDO EMERSON

For some to gaze at the ocean is the way to peace of heart and mind.

Not all of us have that opportunity.

But all of us have the sky! And its moods are infinitely more varied, more intriguing to the imagination, more filled with wonders, than even the broadest sweep of sea.

"When I look at your heavens," wrote the Psalmist, "the work of your fingers, the moon and stars that you have established; what are human beings that you are mindful of them, mortals that you care for them? Yet you have made them a little lower than God, and crowned them with glory and honor."

To contemplate creation by looking at the sky is to restore our perspective, to see God's handiwork in broad sweep, and perhaps to feel that a creation this intricate, this capable, this mysterious, holds us, and our loved one, in ultimate safety and care.

Beneath the vast expanse of the sky, the panorama of clouds and stars, I can sense the order of the world, and feel secure.

JUNE 25

The future is not yet ours; perhaps it never will be. If it comes, it may come wholly different from what we have foreseen. Let us shut our eyes, then, to that which God hides from us, and keeps in reserve in the treasures of His deep counsels. Let us worship without seeing; let us be silent; let us abide in peace.
            —FRANCOIS DE SALIGNAC DE LA MOTHE FÉNELON

How much time we spend anguishing over a future without the one we love—anticipating all the times we would have expected that person to be present with us, sharing our life.

Yet the future is unknown to us. We ourselves may not be present at these events we look toward anticipating grief. Why spend the energy of our lives on an unknowable future when the present world lies all around us, moment by moment, day by day? There is grief enough here. But we do not need to compound that grief by projecting ourselves into a time beyond our knowledge or control.

I feel a wonderful freedom when I stop imagining my future sadness and live only in the present.

If you love me, let me go.

—SOURCE UNKNOWN

I don't know to whom to ascribe this quotation. It came to me as a variant of a current popular song several months after my daughter's death. It has been my experience over many years that the songs that go through my head are usually telling me something. In this case the tune was for a song with which I was only marginally familiar: "If you love me, let me know." But for me the words were, "If you love me, let me go."

If there is a way, which some have suggested, that the spirits of the dead continue to hover close until they see we are going to be all right, until they feel freed to go, then perhaps, through some flash implant in my spirit, my daughter was telling me something. At the time, I thought of the message in those terms.

It is all conjecture, of course, and who knows whether we are projecting our own needs in these images of What Happens Next or whether we are intuitively onto some truth?

But from whatever source, with whatever corroboration or lack of it, this was a good message for me to hear just then.

Blessings on you, dear departed. I'm hoping to catch up with you, one of these days.

JUNE 27

Since her first grief had brought her fully to birth and wakefulness in this world, an unstinting compassion had moved in her, like a live stream flowing deep underground, by which she knew herself and others and the world.

—WENDELL BERRY

It is a difficult birth—this coming into full wakefulness through grief—and not everyone comes out ennobled. But since the rewards of doing it well are as multitudinous as the stars in the sky, it behooves us to do whatever we can to come through well.

What may it take? Attention to our own needs, our state of mind. Reading. Rest. A willingness to be vulnerable again. Counseling, maybe. Talking with understanding friends. For some, prayer, meditation, participation in a healing community.

What we can be sure of is that we will be different. Whether we will be embittered and sad or compassionate and, in a deep sense, happy is not totally within our power to decide. But the outcome may be more within our power than we think. Like any birth, it has its pains and dangers. But it is new life at stake here—new life!

I will use all the wisdom and power I possess to come through this well.

She taught me that grief is a time to be lived through, experienced fully, and that the heavens will not fall if I give voice to my anger against God in such a time.
—ELIZABETH WATSON

Sometimes it's hard to recognize that anger is part of our grief. Maybe we're angry at the doctors and nurses for not making our loved one well. Or for not alleviating the suffering. Or for not doing a better job of keeping us informed.

Maybe we're angry at the loved one—for not trying hard enough to get well, or for not taking better care of himself or herself. Or just for leaving us. Maybe we're angry with ourselves. Or angry at God.

Even when we don't hold a particular person—or God—responsible for the death of our loved one, we're angry. Our life has been disrupted. We have been deprived of something—even if it's only peace—that we wanted.

As with other aspects of grief, we need to recognize anger and express it. We may need to be careful with relatives and friends. But we don't need to worry about God—we can let it fly.

My anger is legitimate, and will burn away sooner if I acknowledge and express it.

JUNE 29

The day goes by like a shadow o'er the heart,
With sorrow, where all was delight.
—STEPHEN FOSTER

Sometimes it's hard to remember how life felt to us before this loss came and shifted the ground beneath us as surely as a landslide or an earthquake.

For a while we mark events with a kind of "first time since it happened" syndrome. At first the events are very mundane and immediate—"the first time I went to the grocery store . . . the first time I got the car washed . . . the first time I went to a movie." Then the seasonal milestones come along—"the first Fourth of July . . . the first Thanksgiving . . . the first birthday," and so on. And all of them shadowed by the loss that darkens everything we do, everything that happens.

We wonder whether it will always be so, and if so, how we can bear it.

Our loss will change the constellation of our lives. That fact will not go away. But its edges will soften, and other events will come along to enrich our lives, so that this grief which seems as though it will forever be "front and center" slips into the background tapestry and our hearts are often and profoundly made glad once more.

For a time sorrow takes up the whole landscape, but joy will come again.

He could feel a hand on his shoulder. "All right," he said softly. "All right." He stood at his walker. He could sense eyes staring at him. "Goodbye," he said to the coffin. He turned on his walker and moved away.

It was a day of sun—warm, bright, a soft wind from the west. The earth was green. The sun felt good on his face and hands.

—TERRY KAY

There is often a strange quietness attendant on the rituals of dying, as though creation itself has stilled for this moment of absolute truth.

We may play through our roles in what seems like a daze—except it isn't a daze but a filling of this role of the bereaved. The rituals are old, but for us the experience is new and painful and raw.

So it is well to have rituals and customs to guide us, services to signify what has happened. Besides giving us some context of faith in which to put our loss, rituals and customs help us Know What to Do with all this energy of grief and pain—a security to cling to when one's inner world is in turmoil.

And in the holy distillations of this moment, how we are comforted by the blessing of warm sun, soft wind, the green earth.

Sometimes the simplest moments hold the most profound truths.

July 1

I know well there is no comfort for this pain of parting: the wound always remains, but one learns to bear the pain, and learns to thank God for what He gave, for the beautiful memories of the past, and the yet more beautiful hope for the future.

—MAX MÜLLER

A woman whose life had had many hard times said, "The hardest grief I have had to bear is this temporary separation from my daughter." That she was able, in faith, to view her adolescent daughter's death as a temporary separation surely helped her immeasurably. But of course she longed for her daughter's presence now.

It is foolish to expect to "get over" a serious grief. The pain is always there, the fantasy of what might have been. Over time, I'm sure that for this woman the pain was mixed in with happy memories of the daughter's childhood and adolescence, and also with her anticipation of their ultimate reunion.

So the mosaics of adjustment are laid down. On some days the grief is most noticeable; on others, the happy memories; on others, the hope of reunion burns bright.

As I think about my loss, the strands of grief and memory and hope are mysteriously braided together.

Everyone can master a grief but he that has it.
—WILLIAM SHAKESPEARE

We are usually our own best judge of what we need to be doing as grievers. To be sure, we could often use a nudge from friends—if we're being too reclusive, for instance. Or maybe we need professional counsel, if we know we're just not doing well at all.

But we don't need to take seriously the comments of probably well-meaning but ignorant folk who imply that we are being indulgent or weak in not "getting over it by now"—whether "now" is six months or six years after the loss has occurred. Every grief has its own timetable, which only the griever knows. And usually the journey through grief is slow and often delayed.

Someone once said it takes seven years to adjust to the loss of someone close. So there's no need to apologize if after many months we are still finding grief a major preoccupation. And there is nothing to be ashamed of if a particularly poignant moment reduces us to tears a very long time after our loved one has died.

What to reply when someone says, "It seems to me you should be getting over that by now"?

How about the above quote from Shakespeare? Not only is it an appropriate response, but you'll seem quite the scholar as well!

July 3

One evening I was leafing through a book and my eye fell on a piece of sculpture we had often looked at together . . . I sat there, staring at it in a daze, but I didn't turn the page. Images of the past rose up and I saw a sort of endless movie and heard a song of victory . . . I felt as though I were climbing out of a sucking marsh. I was alone in my room, but I was filling it completely; it seemed different from the way it had been on the other days. I had somehow gone back into gear. I was able once again to contemplate beauty.

—ANNE PHILIPE

Sometimes the beauty of the world seems excruciatingly painful because we are so aware of our loved one's loss of that world. How can we savor the fragrances and sights of life without a stab of pain that our loved one can no longer have these experiences—or share them with us?

So it is a real step—and an indication of our willingness to trust that our loved one is now in better hands than ours—when we can reclaim our eyes and ears and sensations of taste and touch and smell in all their fullness, knowing that is exactly what our loved one would want for us, too.

The beauty of the world in all its fullness is mine to claim.

The evenings were the hardest to bear. The ritual of the hot drink, the lumps of sugar for the two dogs, the saying of prayers—his boyhood habit carried on throughout our married life—the good night kiss. I continued the ritual, because this too lessened pain, and was, in its very poignancy, a consolation.

—DAPHNE DU MAURIER

Rituals—of a formal or informal nature—carry us through some of our most difficult times. For one thing, they help us know what to do or say. They supply us with a form into which we can pour our inchoate energy and grief—the comfort of the customary.

If they are rituals we have shared with the one we love, they have even more power, bringing the presence of the loved one close in the echoes and gestures of things we have done and said together.

And if they are rituals—like the saying of prayers—which have been shared historically by families and by communities of faith—why, then it is as though a whole legion of people gathered around us to support us in our loneliness and sorrow. But, most importantly, there is the presence of the one with whom we have most intimately shared these rituals. We are, indeed, "going through the motions," but they are holy motions.

As I repeat some of the patterns of our life together, I can almost sense the presence of my loved one.

JULY 5

The sorrow for the dead is the only sorrow from which we refuse to be divorced. Every other wound we seek to heal, every other affliction to forget; but this wound we consider it a duty to keep open; this affliction we cherish and brood over in solitude.

—WASHINGTON IRVING

Perhaps we are affronted by this suggestion—a sort of blame-the-victim parry that makes it seem we are exploiting our grief, clinging to it when we could consider it finished and done.

Are there benefits to us in grieving? Consider:

We get a lot of attention and sympathy from friends.

Grief can be an excuse—to ourselves and others—not to continue with responsibilities we'd as soon be without.

Grief—here's the tough one—can make us feel we have stayed close to the one we loved. After all, the loved one's dying was our last connection, and why wouldn't we want to hold on?

Sympathy from friends is wonderful and we need it. But try a grief support group. They know our need, and will help us know if we're clinging to grief for attention's sake.

Yes, we want to stay close to the one we've lost, but it's the *person* we need to hold in our minds. Dwelling on the loss can get in the way of our doing that.

My hope is found in my love, not in the degree of my grieving.

When we start at the center of ourselves, we discover something worthwhile extending toward the periphery of the circle. We find again some of the joy in the now, some of the peace in the here, some of the love in me and thee which go to make up the kingdom of heaven on earth.

—G. F. SEAR

Our thoughts are so much with the one who is gone. We brood about the person, remember times together, think about the meaning of death. Suppose, for a time, we lay all that aside and return to living in our own skin— breathing deeply, trying to get a sense of our own center.

Not only does this return us to ourselves, it helps us see more clearly the context in which we live. Yes, there are chunks of our lives that are lonely, bereaved. But if we look out on life from our own center, we see there are other aspects on which our sorrow doesn't impinge as heavily. The air we breathe isn't filtered through our sadness. The children playing in the field exude an authentic joy that can be catching.

This takes self-discipline. The temptation is always to be sucked back into grief, but it may help us to "try on" a view of the world in which grief is one part, but not all.

I have some control over how much I let sadness rule my life.

JULY 7

For we have shared many griefs, but they are translated into pure love and rejoicing when we meet.

—MAY SARTON

What makes our hearts rise with joy when we meet again people with whom we have shared a sorrow?

We have all heard of the guilt of the survivor—the person who wonders why he or she has been spared when someone else has perished.

Perhaps there's such a thing, after some time for healing has passed, as the joy of the survivor—not in any gloating or triumphant way, but in simple acknowledgment that, having come through severe testing and anguish, one is alive and has been able to modulate that grief into a life that is productive and to a large degree joyful. We have passed through fire and not been destroyed. We have, in fact, been reborn. Because when our loved one died, something in us died, too—some expectation or hope of a future together. And out of the ashes of that destroyed dream we have been lifted into new life.

And when we find someone for whom this is also true—especially if that is someone with whom we have shared grief in the past—why, of course we are filled with love and rejoicing! What else?

In the fellowship of those reborn out of grief, all are sisters and brothers.

In desperate hope I go and search for her in all the cor-
ners of my house. I find her not.

My house is small and what once has gone from it can
never be regained.

But infinite is thy mansion, my lord, and seeking her I
have come to thy door.

—RABINDRANATH TAGORE

In the course of our life we go to the places we have been
with our loved one—and at each place feel afresh the pang
of our loss.

I remember after my daughter died that I would often
measure the degree of my courage or despair by how far
open I left the door to her room. Almost closed meant a
very bad day—I could scarcely bear to see her familiar
setting. As the months wore on, I was able to leave the
door farther open, and then, of course, to let it stand fully
open against the wall. I am bemused now thinking about
it, but at the time, there was nothing bemusing about it. I
was acting out a desperate struggle not to be overcome.

But those places we come upon, or avoid, are not home
to our loved ones anymore. Searching for them, we come
to the door of the Unknown, which we can enter only in
fantasy. Can we trust that within, One who knows better
than we is caring for them?

In the universe we share, I trust that my loved one is safe.

JULY 9

Real grief is not healed by time . . . If time does anything, it deepens our grief. The longer we live, the more fully we become aware of who she was for us, and the more intimately we experience what her love meant for us. Real, deep love is, as you know, very unobtrusive, seemingly easy and obvious, and so present that we take it for granted. Therefore, it is often only in retrospect—or better, in memory—that we fully realize its power and depth. Yes, indeed, love often makes itself visible in pain.
—HENRI NOUWEN

At first this is frightening. Grief deepening? Am I never going to feel better?

So much of the meaning of our loved one's life becomes distilled, sifted through memory and through experience after his or her death. New insights awaken, new appreciations, and with these come new birth pangs, and new yearnings that our beloved was still with us.

But this ongoing process also promises that, in a way, loved ones will never leave us, that their lives will continue to nourish and, yes, change us—that they will, indeed, be with us always in the mutual interdependence of love.

My loved one will be with me in these bittersweet moments of deepening relationship.

I am slowly, painfully discovering that my refuge is not found in my mother, my grandmother, or even the birds of Bear River. My refuge exists in my capacity to love. If I can learn to love death then I can begin to find refuge in change.

—Terry Tempest Williams

At first it seems a preposterous suggestion—"learn to love death"? Death, which most of the time, to most of us, seems The Enemy?

Perhaps what we are being asked to do—sensitized as we are by our grief—is to love The Truth, to love all that is. So, from full hearts, perhaps we can include in the sweep of our love even that which has caused us great pain.

If we can, then we can stop being imprisoned behind walls of denial and anger; we can stop banging our heads and our hands against what cannot be changed. We can accept what has happened, and relish the life that we have.

I will try to open my hands—and my heart—to life as it is now.

JULY 11

Hikers refer to them as "middle-miles." These are the most exhausting, challenging miles on the path, when the exhilaration of beginning the journey has evaporated into drudgery and the promise of the path's end has not yet given new energy for the stepping.

—HENRY E. WOODRUFF

The journey through grief is very different from the climb up a heroic mountain. Yet there are stages of that ascent which remind us of our own climb out of the valley of despair. In the early days and weeks of our grieving we usually have much to help us—the solicitude of friends, the gathering around of our religious community, the profferings of help.

Then we are in for the long haul, when we are at least as sad but more on our own. We wonder whether we shall ever feel our old energy and hunger for life again. We observe that people who have been grieving do feel better. We are told we will, too, and in our heads maybe we believe it. But the days and weeks drag on and we don't see any infusion of light and joy.

Like the climbers in the "middle-miles," we must keep going, knowing that one day we will get on top of our lives again. Looking back, we'll marvel at how far we've come.

I believe in the top of the mountain even when I can't see it.

Grief teaches the steadiest minds to waver.

—SOPHOCLES

Don't we know it! Sometimes we can't seem to decide the simplest thing. Or we decide and then agonizingly reflect on the decision: was it wise? We rename all the alternatives, chasing them around as though the decision were not already irrevocably made.

It's no wonder. Our world has become suddenly disordered by the death of our loved one, so why wouldn't disorder spread over everything else? The wonder is that we are able to act systematically about anything, not that we occasionally get confused.

This will pass, of course. We will begin to feel grounded again. In the meantime, we can accept this time of flux and try to postpone major decisions—or get friends to consult with us about them. In the early stages of grief is no time to sell the house or decide on a major vocational change!

Of course my mind sometimes plays tricks on me. I'll regain my steadiness and good sense after a while.

JULY 13

He'd begun to wake up in the morning with something besides dread in his heart. Not happiness exactly, not eagerness for the new day, but a kind of urge to be eager, a longing to be happy.

—JON HASSLER

It comes upon us so gradually that we scarcely recognize the change—this moving out of the valley of despair, where the future looks perpetually grim, into a more pleasant land. Then one day we may think to ourselves, *Wait a minute. This feels different!* For now, instead of a sorrowful landscape marked by only occasional moments of happiness, we realize we inhabit a land where we are happy and content more of the time than not. The periods of desolation are now the exception, not the rule.

Without knowing it, we have slipped into a new country. This will take some getting used to. Of course we'll have relapses, which are really not relapses at all but a way of continuing to deepen the grooves in the brain that tell us who we are, now that our loved one has gone. But the shift is a matter for astonishment and gratitude, and sometimes for a quiet waiting to see what other wisdom and self-knowledge may come to us.

I welcome, as a blessing from my loved one, the return of light and joy to my life.

We are healed of a suffering only by experiencing it to the full.

—MARCEL PROUST

There is no skirting around the suffering of grief. If we are to incorporate this event into our lives, we must walk through the center of our suffering, with our eyes open.

We may be tempted to do otherwise—to save ourselves from this pain.

It doesn't work. What we try to avoid will stay, demanding its due, the pain compounding like unpaid interest as we add to the burden of loss the burden of trying to hold the pain at bay.

To be sure we can take "breathers" as we're able—and we need to, to keep our emotional health intact. It is a fine balancing act—when to seek diversion and when to let the full measure of loss declare itself.

We find this out by trial and error. When the pressure begins to build—a sense of being pushed by an unspoken agenda—it's time to release that pressure by being present to our sadness. We don't have to do it alone. Sometimes a friend can listen, without trying to gloss over our grief or burden us with well-meaning advice. A grief group is especially helpful—people who understand that we need to talk about it—again and again and again.

I will be present to my grief; it is my only way to new life.

JULY 15

When I lay [my] questions before God I get no answer. But a rather special sort of No answer. It is not the locked door. It is more like a silent, certainly not uncompassionate, gaze. As though He shook His head not in refusal but in waiving the question. Like, "Peace, child; you don't understand."

—C. S. LEWIS

Sometimes it seems our greatest hope is that we *don't* understand. Because from the vantage we have when we are feeling low, the sense of the futility of life, and the apparent finality of death, can all but overwhelm us.

Far better to acknowledge that our understanding is limited, to relish the stories of faith and intuition that come to us—and wait and see! We stand so close. What if someone trying to view Michelangelo's magnificent painting of "The Creation of Adam" in the Sistine Chapel got so close that all he could see was two fingertips touching? A good view, but a very small piece of the whole picture.

Our questions are unanswerable. The real question is one of trust.

If we can choose where to cry, at home or with a few people who will be fully understanding, perhaps we will feel easier. But if we can't—if we are in church and a hymn catches us off guard, or at a football game and we remember being there with a son or daughter now gone—well, the earth is our home and we can cry where we want.

—MARTHA WHITMORE HICKMAN

Among the extra burdens we do not need when we are dealing with grief is the burden of abiding by some code of when and where it is okay to cry. We are somehow embarrassed if we find ourselves overtaken by grief in a public place.

What are we trying to prove?

When was the last time you saw someone overcome by tears and thought less of that person?

If you see a stranger on the verge of tears, what is your reaction?

See! We are quite willing to extend empathy to a stranger, but less willing to allow ourselves to be the recipients of empathy from others.

Well, then! We are in this world together, and our hearts move toward the one who is sad.

Can we not extend the same courtesy to ourselves?

I will freely give myself permission to cry—even in public!

JULY 17

Sometimes we wish for dreams of our loved one, as a way
of keeping in touch. Sometimes they may be frightening.
But probably they are to be trusted.

Soon after my daughter died from a head injury in-
curred in a fall, I dreamed of standing on the upper deck
of a ship and watching two orderlies carry a stretcher up
the stairway toward me. On the stretcher was a young
woman. She was unconscious, her head bent to one side.
The two men brought her close to where I stood waiting.
They assured me she was going to be fine, and pointed
out that downstairs, on a lower deck, was a picnic table,
with people gathered around. I looked. The people were
the rest of my family and they were looking up, waiting
for me to come and join them, which I did.

The mood of the dream was quite matter-of-fact, quite
serene. I was startled, in thinking of it, at how specific it
was—its message clear: *she is all right. Return to the living,
who need you.*

My dreams are a means of understanding and growth.

I was wholly at peace, at ease and at rest, so that there was nothing upon earth which could have afflicted me.

This lasted only for a time, and then I was changed . . . I felt there was no ease or comfort for me except faith, hope and love, and truly I felt very little of this. And then presently God gave me again comfort and rest for my soul . . . And then again I felt the pain, and then afterwards the delight and the joy, now the one and now the other, again and again, I suppose about twenty times.

—JULIAN OF NORWICH

Just when we think we have ourselves in hand and are going to be able to manage this, we are suddenly plunged into despair again. What happened to our carefully nurtured poise, the confidence we felt ten minutes ago?

The best thing to do is just to ride it out, knowing that in time we'll be on the upswing again—for a while. It is comforting to know that even the saints of the faith had periods of feeling in pain and alone.

After a while these moods will even out, not be so jagged and alarming—though to be a sensitive human being is to be affected by the pain and the joy of life. No need to feel guilty about our low moods. If we can do something to chase them off—fine. If not—wait; they will pass.

I accept my mood swings as part of the process of healing.

JULY 19

Over the nowhere arches the everywhere.
—MARIA RAINER RILKE

I remember on a very cold day retracing my steps in what could have been no more than a square quarter mile of a section of Minneapolis. It was late afternoon, in winter. I could see the top of the building I wanted to get to, but turning toward it, I would again lose sight of it as I hurried among the intervening buildings. I knew that if only I could look down on it from above, I could understand the scheme of streets and find my way.

Sometimes when we are grieving we feel as though we are randomly moving about (or being moved), totally out of touch with any overarching reality or meaning in our lives. Or maybe the feeling is akin to losing one's place in a book. How can we find the page again, and pick up the story line?

For a while we probably can't. Our loss is so consumingly center stage we can't see beyond it, or around it.

We need to be patient with ourselves. We will, in time, be able to find our way through the mazes, be able to pay attention once more to the other parts of our life's story. But there is no use rushing, or no need. The "everywhere" which hovers over the "nowhere" will not disappear. When we're ready, we'll see it.

Even when I can't see the sun, I know that it's there.

It is as if the intensity of grief fused the distance between you and the dead. Or perhaps, in reality, part of one dies. Like Orpheus, one tries to follow the dead on the beginning of their journey. But one cannot, like Orpheus, go all the way, and after a long journey one comes back. If one is lucky, one is reborn.

—ANNE MORROW LINDBERGH

When companions of the way are suddenly gone from the scene, the urge is to follow.

So we set out. If where they have gone is into death, why, we will try to follow them there. Not, in most cases, by suicide, but in the imagination—follow them "across the river," "through the gates of Heaven," into the luminous world of the spirit.

After a while we realize the search is futile. We are lost in a wood, calling for them and they are not there.

It is a turnaround of enormous significance to abandon that search, to return to this world. To speak of this as rebirth is no exaggeration. We have left a demiworld that leads nowhere and have, as changed people, resumed our commitment to life.

My resolve to live "one day at a time" also means "one world at a time." But where my loved one is, a fragment of my spirit lives, and waits.

JULY 21

. . . All those who try to go it sole alone,
Too proud to be beholden for relief,
Are absolutely sure to come to grief.

—ROBERT FROST

Those who, out of pride or for any other reason, try to go it alone are in for a hard time.

Nowhere is this more true than in dealing with the loss of a loved one. We are already lonely—for the one we have lost. To be sure, no one can fill that particular space—and we wouldn't want anyone to—but that emptiness does make us more needful of loving and supporting relationships in the rest of our lives.

The work of grief is hard work, and we need people to help us—to listen, to hold us, to remember our loved one with us, to give us their wisdom.

There is a story of a little girl who got home from visiting her friend later than her mother had expected. When her mother asked the reason for the delay, the child said, "I was helping Jane. Her doll broke."

The mother asked, "Did you help her fix it?"

The child said, "No. I helped her cry."

We all need people to help us cry.

To live in the religious spirit is not easy; the believer is continually on a deep sea 70,000 fathoms deep . . . It is a *great* thing floating on 70,000 fathoms of water and beyond all human aid to be happy: it is a little thing and not at all religious to swim in shallow water with a host of waders . . . No matter how long the religious man lies out there, it does not mean that little by little he will reach land again. He can become quieter, attain a sense of security, love jests and the merry mind. But to the last moment, he lies over 70,000 fathoms of water.

—SÖREN KIERKEGAARD

When we have lost a loved one, we are especially attuned to the world of the spirit. At the same time there is a sense of being cut loose from our moorings. We are, figuratively speaking, "at sea."

Perhaps these words of Kierkegaard can help. We are, indeed, afloat over deep water, with all our questions about the meaning of life, the nature of death. We were never in control, though perhaps we thought we were.

Then, after a while, with our questions still spinning in our heads, we learn to trust the sea—that it is buoyant and will bear our weight.

◆◆

I will rest back on the ocean of unknowing, trusting that I can ride its swells and its troughs without peril.

People in mourning have to come to grips with death before they can live again. Mourning can go on for years and years. It doesn't end after a year; that's a false fantasy. It usually ends when people realize that they can live again, that they can concentrate their energies on their lives as a whole, and not on their hurt, and guilt, and pain.

—ELISABETH KÜBLER-ROSS

No one is asking us to forget, to turn away from all that we loved and cherished in the one we have lost. We couldn't do that even if we wanted to.

The task before us—and it can take a very long time—is to incorporate this grief and loss into the rest of our lives, so that it doesn't continue to dominate our lives. It's no longer the first thing we think of when we wake up in the morning, or the last thing we relinquish before we sleep.

A child said to his mother, in regard to the outpouring of kindnesses after his father's death, "There are so many good things. There's just one bad thing."

The "bad thing" will always be there, but when it begins to take its place among the good things life offers, we're on our way.

Even in my sadness I will be open to new adventure.

My heart is in anguish within me . . .
And I say, "O, that I had wings like a dove!
   I would fly away and be at rest."

—PSALM 55:4-6

Even in our "normal life" there are times when we'd like
to fly away, be gone to some place free from the stress
we're under. Now, when reminders of our loss greet us at
every turn, the urge to flee can seem overwhelming.

We have probably all known of people who have tried.
As a small child, I overheard my father say of a family
friend who had become an alcoholic, "He didn't start to
drink at all until his son died." An attempt to flee.

Or we read of someone who commits suicide: "She had
been despondent since the death of her husband."

Going through grief ourselves, we can understand this
desperation, though such recourses solve nothing and only
increase the anguish of family and friends.

But we may need a temporary respite—a trip, maybe.
Perhaps some change of routine. Even a new job. A few
months after my daughter's death, I took on a part-time
job in the afternoons in addition to my freelance writing.
I kept it for five years. I remember driving myself to work
on the first afternoon and already feeling the lift of doing
something new, in a community of friendly people.

I will choose my flights carefully—but where might I go?

July 25

I had to struggle alone, and all I knew was that Father's
death caused me to ask questions for which I could find
no answer, and I was living in a world which believed
that all questions are answerable. I, too, believe that all
questions are answerable, but not in scientific terms, or
in the language of provable fact.

—MADELEINE L'ENGLE

We will be like cats chasing our tails if we expect to answer with rational answers all the questions death brings
to us.

Well, where are the answers, if not in fact?

Maybe in a sudden sense of peace on a troubled afternoon.

Or in an unexpected visit and a warm hug from a friend
who says, "I was nearby and I just wondered how you're
doing."

Maybe in the rustle of trees on an otherwise still afternoon.

Or in a story told of a near-death experience which
transforms a person's life.

Or in some words in a book that seem meant just for
you.

My spirit picks up clues my mind might pass right by.

Illness is the night-side of life, a more onerous citizenship.
Everyone who is born holds dual citizenship, in the king-
dom of the well and in the kingdom of the sick.
—SUSAN SONTAG

One of the reasons the death of someone close is so profoundly shaking for us is that it holds up the mirror to us
and says, *You, too.* Sometimes this may seem a welcome
prospect—our wish to join the loved one is to strong, and
our aversion to life without that person is so great.

Yet there is a way in which we draw back from facing
our own vulnerability and the prospect of our own death.
We read of death daily, sometimes skirt close to it in our
own and our loved ones' illnesses, but when it enters the
portals of our own family and close friendships, it speaks
in a different, more intimate language. The mysteries and
quandaries of death ask their recurrent questions: Is there
life beyond? Do we know one another in a personal way?
Do we know ourselves? Or do we become a part of some
great cosmic energy?

There are no sure answers to these questions. The best
answer—as the best memorial to our loved one—is to live
our lives fully, one day at a time.

◆◆

*I am a citizen of this day. Tomorrow will bring its own demands,
its own gifts.*

JULY 27

Hell, Madame, is to love no longer.
—GEORGES BERNANOS

Of course we miss the expressions of love from the one we have lost. And our love for that person, too, goes on and on. Where can we put it? We direct it into the air, hoping somehow it will find its target.

Things could be worse! Imagine what it would be like if, in our grieving, not only were we unable to love the one who is gone, but we couldn't respond with overflowing hearts to the dear ones who come to comfort us.

Music has been called a universal language. Love is another. But it takes constant replenishment, and fortunate are we if our experience has been such that we can be among the replenishers of that love.

As we grieve over our physical separation from our loved one, perhaps we can think of that person and ourselves as surrounded by a love in which the entire creation lives and moves and has its being.

Perhaps, especially in my sorrow, I can reach out in love to others.

God, bless to me the new day,
Never vouchsafed to me before;
It is to bless Thine own presence
Thou hast given me this time, O God.

—CELTIC PRAYER

When we are grieving it is hard to see a new day as a fresh opportunity for life and growth. We carry such baggage of sorrow with us. Sorrow burdens all that we do, all that we think about. So it is only by an act of will that we can even try to think of this day as a fresh start, a new opportunity.

But try. One way to begin is to concentrate, not on ourselves, but on the hours ahead as though they were unknown visitors, and on whatever name we give to the source of life that has endowed us with life and love and beauty, and with precious relationships.

Sit in some quiet place and close your eyes and, breathing deeply, try to get in touch with the deepest stillness within yourself—a place of wordless tranquility. Then you might repeat slowly to yourself the prayer at the top of this page. Name to yourself the hours of the day. If you know what you'll be doing at a given time, try to project some of this peace onto that activity—as a blessing. Perhaps you will recall this when the hour comes.

May this day be a New Day for me.

JULY 29

Failing to fetch me at first keep encouraged,
Missing me one place search another,
I stop somewhere waiting for you.

—WALT WHITMAN

Where have the dead gone? Where can we find them?

We will wear ourselves out, asking these questions, and yet we do. We look in the last place we saw them. We return to their favorite haunts, hoping for a sense of their presence.

We may find there what we are looking for. And if we do, it may make us sad, or happy.

There is no predicting. People tell of encountering the spirits of loved ones at places they had visited together—or at places with which they have had no connection at all.

Sometimes it seems they are notable only for their absence. Sometimes it seems we can almost call them forth. And sometimes they surprise us.

A friend tells me how, sitting alone in a church, playing the organ, he was visited several months after her death by the presence of a young woman, a presence so strong that after a while he stopped his playing and said, "All right, Mary Beth." Then, he says, "I felt her smile."

Dear love. I wait for you. Do you wait for me?

In the point of rest at the center of our being, we encounter a world where all things are at rest in the same
way. Then a tree becomes a mystery, a cloud a revelation, each man a cosmos of whose riches we can only
catch glimpses. The life of simplicity is simple, but it opens
to us a book in which we never get beyond the first syl-
lable.

—DAG HAMMARSKJÖLD

Simplicity is not the tenor of life for most of us. We rush
around tending to work, to household, to family and
friends. But there are times, particularly after we have
been through some pivotal experience—like the death of
a loved one—when we are conscious of "the point of rest
at the center of our being."

Whom do we meet there? The Christian tradition speaks
of "the communion of saints," by which is meant not only
those who have lived unblemished lives (a very small
gathering!), but all who have lived and died—or are living
now—and even the souls of the yet unborn.

Each of us has his or her own chosen community of
love, and we may find some healing, some rest, if in quiet
interludes we can settle into that "center of our being" and
call to us the spirits of our loved ones.

In the community of love, all are at home.

July 31

Pain—has an Element of Blank—
It cannot recollect
When it began—or if there were
A time when it was not—

—EMILY DICKINSON

When we are suffering intense grief, it is almost hard to remember what it felt like to be happy. Particularly when loss comes suddenly, it is as though we have been shunted into a different world where nothing has the same meaning it had before. In fact, we are startled, offended almost, that people seem to be conducting business as usual.

I recall going to the dentist soon after my daughter's death and hearing almost with incredulity the banal chit-chat of people in the waiting room. *How could they? Didn't they know?*

Of course, we will not always be at this point of Altered Reality. We will, in time, incorporate our loss into our lives so that it is part of the daily background of living. Though it is sad, it doesn't shock and startle us with each new day.

And maybe our initial inability to remember how it felt to be happy was for the good after all—the contrast would have been too painful. Besides, we needed to give our attention to what was going on where we were.

I will be present to the moment as each day unfolds.

Faith is a way of waiting—never quite knowing, never quite hearing or seeing, because in the darkness we are all but a little lost. There is doubt hard on the heels of every belief, fear hard on the heels of every hope.
—FREDERICK BUECHNER

We recognize ourselves here—"all but a little lost." Because we can never really be sure for long that the particulars of our faith, our hope, are what we would like to believe they are. But not quite lost, either. Because as sunshine follows rain follows sunshine, faith, as it waits, moves from confidence into doubt into confidence again. So, in a comforting solidarity with the rest of the waiting faithful, we make our conjectures, hope our hopes.

And every once in a while some minor miracle of insight and confidence, some serendipity with no explanation other than grace, renews us, and we are willing to relinquish our need to know the details. Instead, we trust that all shall be well.

I will wait in faith, trusting that One I cannot know, knows and cares for me.

AUGUST 2

We cannot do everything at once but we can do something at once.

—CALVIN COOLIDGE

When we are grieving we are often beset by a kind of lassitude. We feel flattened, devoid of energy. It's all we can do to get through the day and fall into bed hoping for the oblivion of sleep.

It's fine to take some time to rest, to let the wells of energy and resolve begin to fill up again. But what if, many months later, we are still dragging, still lethargic?

It is important to know what is going on. Barring illness (which we should always check for—people who are grieving have a disproportionate chance of getting sick), perhaps our lethargy is a form of denial: if I don't *move*, maybe it won't be so.

It is hard to shake loose of such a feeling. But we can, by starting with one thing. Buying some seeds to plant a garden. Baking bread. Visiting a neighbor. Anything to break the logjam of inactivity. It may seem as fateful as that first "giant step" out of the capsule and into space.

I cannot bear to look down the long road of years without my loved one. But I don't have to. I have today. And I will, today, do one new thing.

Is there no pity sitting in the clouds,
That sees into the bottom of my grief?
—WILLIAM SHAKESPEARE

Grief is one of the great common experiences of human
beings, and yet sometimes we feel so alone in our sadness.
Even when family members share the same loss, the grief
is different for each one. Our history with the person is
different. Our place in the family constellation is different.
We are of different temperaments. Sometimes our very
closeness to one another makes the differences in the way
we express grief hard to understand. Yet we long for common understanding.

Or do we? Our grief may be in common, but it is private
as well. Our loss is unique, our own turf. No one can feel
just as we feel.

Well, is there some other force—some "pity sitting in
the clouds"? Some god? Some force of nature? Again, it is
our longing to be known, to be accepted, to be comforted.

In time we will find solace, as we walk around and
around this grief, walk through the middle of it, look at it
from every angle. But we can do that only if we know that
beyond our fingertips, our friends and loved ones are loving us, wishing us well. As we do for them.

◆◆

*I have what I need to see my way through this—if you, my
friends, are with me.*

AUGUST 4

Nothing can fill the gap when we are away from those we love, and it would be wrong to try and find anything. We must simply hold out and win through. That sounds hard at first, but at the same time it is a great consolation, since leaving the gap unfilled preserves the bond between us. It is nonsense to say that God fills the gap; he does not fill it, but keeps it empty so that our communion with another may be kept alive, even at the cost of pain.
—DIETRICH BONHOEFFER

It is strangely reassuring—this suggestion that the pain of that empty space will always be with us. Because while we do want to feel better, we do not want, ever, to forget.

We will, of course, find new places to put the affection and love and time that we used to pour out to the one we lost. Not to do that would be to turn inward, refuse to be vulnerable—a poor memorial, a poor stewardship of the life left to us.

But our ability to love and care is not limited to some finite number, so that taking on a new love means replacing an old one. Time does not expand, but love does—as with a parent who has three children, and then has another.

What was once loved and cherished is not replaceable.

Dear _____, There is a space in my heart that is always yours.

My wife of 57 years was buried today beside our son, who died in 1941 as a result of a truck accident when he was hitchhiking to take a job. She has longed for him all these years and now she is with him. I know they are embraced in happiness.

—TERRY KAY

Do you think of it—who might be there, welcoming your loved one? Elisabeth Kübler-Ross, the Swiss-born psychiatrist who has done so much work on death and dying, says she believes none of us dies alone—that our loved ones come to greet us, to welcome us to the other side.

I remember, when my daughter died, thinking how she and my father, who had died a little more than a year earlier, might be rejoicing in each other. My heart was torn, and for a while I almost wanted to be with them. It was a long time ago, and now I am in no particular hurry. But someday . . . I think, when I am feeling confident in my faith and recalling the loved ones I have lost . . . someday I shall be part of that joyous reunion, too.

It is a hope I cherish—to rejoin my loved ones.

AUGUST 6

> Those who grieve find comfort in weeping and in arousing their sorrow until the body is too tired to bear the inner emotions.
>
> —MAIMONIDES

Perhaps the value of very overt expressions of grief—wailing, lamenting, screaming—is that one gets quite worn out and a kind of temporary anesthesia sets in.

There is much to be said for this over the "stiff upper lip" practice of some settings, where so much demonstrativeness may be considered bizarre and self-indulgent.

Strange as it may seem at first if we are not used to it (we will be startled at the sound of our own voice), it can be very helpful to raise our voice against the faceless enemy, even though we know no one is going to answer and give us back our loved one.

So maybe it's worth trying. If you'd rather wail in private, fine. Just find a space isolated enough that you can't be heard, and "let fly" all that pent-up grief and anger.

Feel guilty about ranting against God? Not to worry—God can take it.

By discovering my own inwardness I am in communion
with all other human beings, with nature and beauty and
the goodness of all that is.

—MARIA BOULDING

In our grief, sometimes we feel so alone, as though fate
has singled us out for this misfortune and we have no
companions, no one whose experience of the world even
touches ours.

While our situation is in some ways unique—as unique
as the person we have lost—perhaps we can find comfort
in realizing how profoundly we are a part of the great
human story. And not only the human story. For life in
all its forms is a cycle of birth, living, death, rebirth. Even
the mountains rise up, are eroded flat, and rise up again.

In contemplative silence we can sense communion with
all people, and with trees, flowers, wind, sky. I remember
how, in the anguished months after my daughter died, I
would step out into my backyard and commune with the
trees—laying my hands against the bark. Sometimes
(when I was sure no one was looking!) I put my arms
around a favorite tree, and rested against it, as though the
common source of life that fed us both would bring me
strength and stability.

◆◆

*I am a part of all that is. The great mystery of creation holds
me at its heart—as it holds my lost love. In this we are together.*

AUGUST 8

She thought that she had never before had a chance to realize the might, grimness and tenderness of God. She thought that now for the first time she began to know herself, and she gained extraordinary hope in this beginning of knowledge.

—JAMES AGEE

If we have ever wondered about the limits of our strength and our ability to endure, our experience of loss will tell us much. Our life is shaken to the foundation. But we survive. And out of this terrible, rarefied self-knowledge comes, if we are fortunate, a kind of empathy with all of creation—a sense of the wonder at the suffering and the beauty, of the world. We know ourselves to be in this world, to be part of it and also that it is out of our hands. We cannot manage any of it, but we are in the hands of One who can.

In this purifying and terrible wisdom, may I feel the regenerating presence of God, for consolation, and for hope.

I tell you hopeless grief is passionless.
—ELIZABETH BARRETT BROWNING

One of the many moods of grief is a kind of numbness, a despair so deep and pervasive that nothing seems able to ripple its surface. This is perhaps a benign form of anesthesia, giving our senses time to rest a bit before we reenter the whirlpool of torn lives, of shattered dreams, of anguished tears.

As with all other moods of grief, it will pass. Something else—perhaps easier to bear, perhaps harder—will take its place.

To know this is more than just a stoic acceptance of what is. It is to be reminded that there are seasons of grieving—and like a plunge into frost after some balmy days of spring, or like a day of Indian summer, these mini-seasons are not predictable. But they will pass, and they have their own inner logic. Sometimes the best we can do is say, "Okay. That's how it is today. What can I do that is most compatible with this mood?" and go on about whatever business—or lack of it—the day calls forth. As for tomorrow—who knows?

Unless I bind it to me, hopelessness doesn't last forever.

AUGUST 10

I have come to believe in the "Sacrament of the Moment," which presupposes trust in the ultimate goodness of my creator.

—RUTH CASEY

We dwell so much on the past when we are grieving—the immediate past—the occasion of death itself, and then the happier days when our loved one was with us in all his or her strength.

And then we dwell on the future—the deprivation it will be to face those years without our loved one.

But the present moment is all any of us have—even this present moment, when you are reading these words.

As you have chosen this moment to read these words, choose another moment and live in its intensity alone, without swerving into either the past or the future. You may be surprised at how much lighter you feel, how much freer to appreciate the life that is going on around you.

To make such a choice is to acknowledge your own inability to repeat the past or to control the future. It is also a gesture of trust in a Creator in whose hands are all times and all places.

This moment is unique in all of my life and I will appreciate it for itself.

The relationships of our life are a system, an interlocking network, and when one element is affected, so are they all. The death of a [loved one] will unbalance the whole lot . . . It is a good time to pay attention, to make these relationships as good as possible. If we are buoyed and fed by satisfying relationships now, there is less other-directed energy floating around, trying to attach in unrealistic ways to the one who is gone.

—MARTHA WHITMORE HICKMAN

It is well known that after the loss of a loved one, a person's resistance to physical illness is often lowered. It is also true that such a loss can bring to the surface existing weaknesses in the emotional relationships within the family. In a case as extreme as the death of a child, one expert estimates that 75 percent of the marriages in which the death occurs experience serious trouble within a year.

So we would be well advised to watch for danger signals and, if we sense serious trouble, to seek professional help. We have lost enough already—and if we can negotiate the shoals and rapids of this experience, our relationships not only will survive, but will be stronger and richer for what we have been through together.

In going through this rough time, I will face honestly what other strains it may expose in the fabric of my life, and consider getting help if I need it.

AUGUST 12

O Great Spirit,
Whose voice I hear in the winds,
And whose breath gives life to all the world,
hear me! I am small and weak, I need your
strength and wisdom.

—NATIVE AMERICAN PRAYER

To whom shall we turn in our sorrow?

We have many choices, and need different kinds of comfort and reassurance at different times.

Sometimes we need other people.

Sometimes we need our own solitude.

And sometimes the world of nature speaks a healing word. Seasons follow upon one another and return—with new leaves, new blossoms. Water is drawn up into the sky, becomes clouds, then returns to us as rain and snow to fill our rivers and lakes. Stars sprinkle the sky in discernible patterns, though they are light-years away.

Something is going on here that speaks of a wisdom greater than we know. The breath of the Creator is all around us, wrapping us in warmth and life.

Everything changes; nothing is lost.

. . . you will not be cured, but . . . one day—an idea that will horrify you now—this intolerable misfortune will become a blessed memory of a being who will never again leave you. But you are in a stage of unhappiness where it is impossible for you to have faith in these reassurances.

—MARCEL PROUST

It is hard to believe, when we are in the midst of heavy grief, that any good will come of this. We may resent any such suggestion—as though someone is trying to offer a palliative too soon, trying to proffer a "bright side" when the whole world is darkened.

It is true that we will never be "cured"—never restored to the being we were before. But we will not be forever bereft. A larger world will present itself, a picture whose frame has suddenly expanded, leapt out, to include more than we had known. And in that expanded sense of our own world will be the presence—and the absence—of the one we love. A more shadowed world, perhaps, but a more luminous world, too.

If I cannot believe it now, I can hold out the hope that in time my lost love will be a continuing blessed presence in my life.

AUGUST 14

There is no way out, only a way forward.
—MICHAEL HOLLINGS

"Is there no relief from this wound?" we wonder. "Is there nowhere I can go to turn aside, to get away?"

What we would like to do, often, is to go back. Go back before the accident. Go back before the illness.

But that world no longer exists. Our grief experience is a watershed and it has cut us off forever from that world which now seems so simple and almost idyllic (though we know better)—the life we knew with our loved one, the life Before This Happened.

Still we keep trying, remembering, wishing until the thought pattern is established in our brain: *this is your world now; this is what your life is like.*

Convinced, bit by bit, we begin to go forward—into a new sense of time and relationships, including a new relationship with the one who has died, and a new relationship with ourselves.

Our other available choice is to stand still, and we may try it for a while. But we know we will turn to stone if we let that happen. No, we must keep moving, and in the only direction that is open to us—forward. Forward into new land, into unknown adventure, unknown territory.

I stand at the threshold of new life. What will I do? I can stand still. Or I can go forward. Those are my choices.

I am reminded that what I adore, admire, and draw from Mother is inherent in the Earth. My mother's spirit can be recalled simply by placing my hands on the black humus of mountains or the lean sands of desert. Her love, her warmth, and her breath, even her arms around me—are the waves, the wind, sunlight, and water.

—TERRY TEMPEST WILLIAMS

What we have lost is not replaceable—is not supplanted by the other manifestations of life around us, no matter how beautiful—any more than the loss of a child is made up for by the birth of another child. And yet . . . and yet . . . perhaps it can give us some comfort to think about the oneness of creation. The words on a poster our daughter had hung in her room shortly before her death began, "The same sun warms us," and went on to say, " . . . and we share each other's lives, lingering in each other's shadows." My husband and I framed the poster, and for many years it hung in my writing room—a source of great comfort.

Can we, in the air that surrounds us, the sunshine that bathes us with its warmth and light, the life that surges in our own being, imagine the abiding presence of our loved one?

AUGUST 16

Like an ant on a stick both ends of which are burning,
 I go to and fro without knowing what to do,
  and in great despair . . .
Graciously look upon me.
Thy love is my refuge. Amen.

—TRADITIONAL PRAYER, INDIA

Someone was once described as "having lost his sense of purpose and therefore redoubled his speed."

Sometimes we are like that—frantically hurrying about in the vain hope that if we are *very* busy, we will somehow anesthetize ourselves and not hurt so much.

There is some point in being busy—one gets tired and is able to sleep. And maybe if we are very busy doing something for others, we will forget our own pain for a while.

But sometimes the activity is purposeless—just a way to keep busy, as though that would take care of it.

But busyness doesn't take care of it, and so despair—as well as physical and emotional fatigue—takes its toll and we are worse off than before.

The source of healing is not rushing around, but that calming assurance that love is at the heart of life, and is both our refuge and the source of our strength to go on.

I will stop my frantic busyness and reconnect with my source of strength.

It was not until the cremation was over, which only my children and a few friends attended, and I had scattered my husband's ashes at the end of the garden where we often walked together, and my children had returned to their own homes, that I knew, with full force, the finality of death . . . What had to be endured must be endured now, and at once, alone.

—DAPHNE DU MAURIER

The timing for facing the aloneness death leaves us with may be different for different people. Maybe right away isn't the best time. And some can't be physically alone for long—as in the case of a grieving mother or father who still must attend to the needs of young children. But in the quiet moments before sleep—or when waking in the night and remembering—each of us is faced with the inescapably solitary aspects of grief.

And why not? While we can talk with others, there is a territory of loss only we can enter. But there is a strange ambiguity in our solitude. Often when we are most desperately confronting our loneliness, the sense of our loved one is strongest. The person is gone; we are desperately lonely. But what is this vitality in the air?

I will step into the unknown dark, trusting I will be safe.

AUGUST 18

If God is, He is everywhere present. He is not an occasional visitor, nor ever more truly present than at this very instant. He is always ready to flow into our heart; indeed, He is there now—it is we who are absent.

—ARTHUR FOOTE

Can we believe that God is present to us in our sorrow? Is with us, as close companion? And wants to be known to us, and wants our peace? And holds our loved one in tender care?

Maybe such a journey of faith is a bit like walking toward home in the dark. There is no light to see by, but we grope our way in this familiar yet unfamiliar world, turning where we know the road turns, moving toward what we know must be there. Though we can't see ahead, the ground beneath our feet feels right, and as we approach a door that surely must be there, someone inside, someone we love, turns on the light to welcome us home.

When I am feeling alone and cut off from all sources of support, I will "try on for size" the possibility that God is with me, and will see me through.

Time elapses differently for the bereaved. It creeps. Every minute had been so fraught, so filled with emotions, events and high drama, that each day had passed like a week.

—RICHARD MERYMAN

One reason the future looms so dark when we are confronted with loss is this slow motion of time. We are like children for whom a next birthday seems a lifetime away—life is not routine at all and there is so much new experience to go through.

Only unlike children for whom unfolding life is potentially full of wonder and surprise, we see ahead a succession of days colored by grief. We know how our first days of grief seemed to take forever. We look ahead and think, Will it always be like that? We cannot bear to think of one week. But a month? A year? A decade, even?

Mercifully, this kind of time expansion will not last. Time will begin to slip away as it did before our loss. The sharp edges of grief will soften and feelings that once struck us like a physical blow will be less frequent. We will be on our way. Time will cease to be our enemy and become our friend again.

◆◆

Today is its own time. Tomorrow's time will be different and I won't try to second-guess it.

AUGUST 20

Eleonora [Duse] said, "Tell me about Deirdre and Patrick," and made me repeat to her all their little sayings and ways, and show her their photos, which she kissed and cried over. She never said, "Cease to grieve," but she grieved with me, and, for the first time since their death, I felt I was not alone.

—ISADORA DUNCAN

How we need to talk about the one we have lost. It not only gives us something to do with the energy of grief, but also establishes the continuity of memory and spirit of one who was so much a part of our lives.

Particularly when young lives are lost—as in the case of Isadora Duncan, whose two young children drowned—to speak of them and their ways somehow extends lives too soon cut off, affirms the reality of their having been here—*See, I will speak of them. They were important. They were here.*

To talk freely of the dead is also to begin to get used to our different experience of them now. We still have a relationship with them. We talk as a way to try it out, and try ourselves out. We miss them. Can we reach across the line of death—back to where they were? Will our memory serve us? Yes, it will. Who are they to us now? It is all so new. We say their names and our minds reverberate with the echoes of a new world.

I will speak of my lost love—one way to learn my new life.

Death is the veil which those who live call life:
They sleep, and it is lifted.

—PERCY BYSSHE SHELLEY

At first this seems to demean the splendid experience of being alive. Who could conceive of wonders beyond those we know—the starlit sky, the fragrance of lilies, the wonder of human love? We embrace the world in all its beauty and delight (and its pain as well, for that is part of what being human is), and when we lose a loved one, we mourn not only for ourselves but on behalf of our loved one—to have lost all this.

Yet people who have reported near-death experiences tell us that they have lost all fear of death. Some of them say they have almost been loath to return, because the glimpse they saw of life beyond death was so much more glorious than anything we know.

Who can know? Not we, bound as we are to the blessings and troubles of being alive. But . . . suppose they are right? And regardless of what we think of those stories, we have the testimony of many religions to the promise of a life after death which is marvelous beyond our imagining.

Life is an adventure whose terms I know. Death is an adventure, too.

AUGUST 22

"To forgive oneself"? No, that doesn't work: we have to *be forgiven*. But we can only believe this is possible if we ourselves can forgive.

—DAG HAMMARSKJÖLD

It is all bound up together—the ability to forgive and the ability to feel forgiven. To be harsh with other people is in some ways a projection of how hard we are on ourselves: if I have to toe the mark, so should you. If I set these high standards for myself, why shouldn't I expect the same from you?

When we have lost a loved one and are hard taskmasters for ourselves, we are setting ourselves up for trouble. Of course there were things we did wrong—harsh words, a promise we weren't able to keep, a visit we planned to make and didn't.

The question now is not—if it ever was—whose "fault" it was, who is justified in complaining or feeling hurt. The question now is, *Can I let it go?* Because if we can, we can be assured that our loved one has already done so.

Requiescat in pace. *May we all "rest in peace."*

Even though I walk through the valley of the shadow of death, I fear no evil; for thou art with me; thy rod and thy staff, they comfort me. Thou preparest a table before me in the presence of mine enemies; thou anointest my head with oil, my cup overflows. Surely goodness and mercy shall follow me all the days of my life; and I shall dwell in the house of the Lord forever.

—PSALM 23:4–6

This Psalm from the Hebrew Scriptures has comforted men and women for centuries. Perhaps it is most often used to comfort people who themselves are facing death. But we who have survived the death of loved ones know that they do not walk through that valley alone. Often it is we who have walked with them—sat by their bedsides, held their hands, shared their sometimes spoken, sometimes unspoken, anxiety and fear. We have often been privileged to hear as well their expressions of faith and trust.

And then they are gone, and we are left. Now it is we who need comfort and reassurance. Perhaps these verses from the Twenty-third Psalm can serve a similar function as we repeat them over and over, until the light begins to shine through and the heart is calmed.

I am grateful for words that heal.

AUGUST 24

In prayer, you encounter God in the soft breeze, in the distress and joy of your neighbor and in the loneliness of your own heart.

—HENRI NOUWEN

What does it mean to pray? Sometimes we think of prayer as being consciously articulated thoughts, petitions, and thanksgivings addressed to God. We speak, or think, and wait for God to answer. But what if prayer is sometimes nothing more than a mood of being attentive to what is going on? Joan Baez has described prayer as Paying Attention.

Perhaps in the mood of Paying Attention, we can welcome God into our lives—our joys and sorrows—as one who is also Paying Attention, and in that attentiveness understands and shares our sorrow, even as God's love wraps us around in God's mystery, and makes us feel we're going to make it home.

God is present in my joy, and in my sorrow.

She sat there and began to learn patience, staring at the
floor, where a dusty track from the door of the sitting-room
to the door of the empty bedroom had been marked by
rough, heavy shoes.

—COLETTE

The writer is describing her mother's attitude in the aftermath of her husband's death. The service is over, the ex-
citement has passed. Now the long learning to Do Without
the presence of the loved one begins.

It is a task demanding the utmost patience, and a willingness to look, again and again, at those paths and places
where the loved one walked, sat, lived, and slept, and does
so no more.

After my grandfather died, when I was eleven, one of
the most heart-wrenching things I recall was seeing his
shoes standing neatly by the closet door. They were black
leather, high-top, lace-up shoes, the leather configured
with creases and bumps that conformed to his feet and his
walking. I was accustomed to seeing them on his feet—
and now they stood empty.

◆◆

*The moods of grief, like the moods of the day or of the year, are
to be honored, and will pass.*

AUGUST 26

Be in the world as if you were a stranger or a traveller:
when evening time comes, expect not the morning; and
when morning time comes expect not the .evening; and
prepare as long as you are in good health for sickness,
and so long as you are alive for death.
      —AN-NAWAWI [FROM MUSLIM SCRIPTURE]

It would indeed be hard to bear if the first intensity of
grief went on and on and on, year after year. But that
doesn't happen. We do begin to feel better. This may startle us. We may even wonder whether we are being disloyal to our love. How foolish! What would our loved one
want more than to see us lifted from our sadness? And
indeed, the truth of who the person was can come to us
much better once some of the grief has passed. In the early
stages we are preoccupied not with the memory of our
loved one, but with our own pain.

Particularly in the early stages of grieving, let's not think
ourselves into a future we cannot know. Whatever else it
is, will surely be different from our frantic imaginings.

A Quaker discourse comes to mind on "being present
where you are." It is good advice at any time, but especially now.

I will try to be present to this day.

Returning from the wilderness [a man] becomes a restorer of order, a preserver. He sees the truth, recognizes his true heir, honors his forebears and his heritage, and gives his blessing to his successors. He embodies the passing of human time, living and dying within the human limits of grief and joy.

—WENDELL BERRY

When we are in the midst of grief, we would never recognize ourselves in these words of Wendell berry. All we recognize is the wilderness.

But after a while—perhaps after a very long time and almost against our will—we recognize that some of the rest of this description fits us, too. While we are not grateful for the experience of loss, we may in time become grateful for the hard-won wisdom it can bring us—that we are, in fact, stronger, wiser, better equipped to deal with life, more helpful to others, more confident of our place and that of our loved one in the human stream.

But it is a wilderness. And there is a way in which it will always call to us: *Come back. Remember how sad you were?*

And we will go back. But we'll go back stronger. And we won't stay as long.

If part of my legacy from sorrow is new strength, I will embrace it. I will not turn away.

AUGUST 28

If death my friend and me divide,
thou dost not, Lord, my sorrow chide,
or frown my tears to see;
restrained from passionate excess,
thou bidst me mourn in calm distress
for them that rest in thee.

—CHARLES WESLEY

Sometimes we have the mistaken notion that people of faith do not grieve. Confident that the essence of their loved one has survived and that they will know each other again, they move calmly through this temporary separation without tears or turmoil.

Not so. Let us not add to our already burdened hearts any further burden of guilt that we so easily "give way" to our grief. Wouldn't we miss our loved one if he or she moved halfway around the world? The imponderable mysteries of death are far more impenetrable than having a loved one move to a foreign land!

Fortunate are those whose faith remains strong in the face of loss. They are also fortunate if they can mourn freely and without recrimination from themselves or others. To be human is to feel the pain of loss. To be healed of that pain is wonderful, but there are no shortcuts. There is only the way through.

I will deal honestly with my pain; we know each other well.

I was in a garden at the Rodin Museum. For a few minutes I was alone, sitting on a stone bench between two long hedges of roses. Pink roses. Suddenly I felt the most powerful feeling of peace, and I had the thought that death, if it means an absorption into a reality like the one that was before me, might be all right.

—IRVING HOWE

What are the sources of epiphanies like this moment described by the eminent literary critic Irving Howe?

The sociologist Peter Berger suggests that gods are not, as some claim, human projections of our wishful thinking, but that humanity and its works—angels, skyscrapers, symphonies—are God's projections into the world. He speaks of an "otherness that lurks behind the fragile structures of everyday life."

We read these statements and conjectures, and our hearts rise. As we wend our way through the shadows and high moments in the wake of loss, these statements and intuitions are as food to the starving, as water to those all but overcome with thirst.

I will watch for my own moments in the garden.

AUGUST 30

Give sorrow words; the grief that does not speak
Whispers the oe'r fraught heart and bids it break.
—WILLIAM SHAKESPEARE

The pressure of unspoken grief is like that inside a pressure cooker—it builds and builds until one feels as though another tiny increment of pain will drive one mad.

Speak. Tell a friend. Tell another friend, or the same friend again. A wise friend will know one must tell this tale again and again.

One way to begin—particularly if death has been unexpected and hard to believe—is to recount to this understanding friend, in as much detail as you can remember, the events of the day on which death occurred. "I got up in the morning. I had my usual breakfast of cereal and juice and coffee. I read the paper"—as mundane as that.

This kind of retelling of the day grounds the event in the real world and helps us begin to believe the terrible truth of that day. What happened is not a fantasy, or something we can put in a bubble and hold away from the rest of our life. It took place in real time, on a real day, and while it will be terribly sad to recount, the recounting will help release the pressure inside and activate the flow of healing—friend to friend.

As often as I need to, I will tell my story.

I believe that God is in me as the sun is in the colour and fragrance of a flower—the Light in my darkness, the Voice in my silence.

—HELEN KELLER

Surely a woman who from birth could neither see nor hear speaks out of a deprivation more profound than anything we can imagine. And yet with the long, persistent—and insistent—care of her teacher and mentor, Anne Sullivan, Helen Keller was able to break from this darkness, to liken the presence of the God within her to wonders she could know through her sense of smell, through warmth on her skin and vibrations of her fingertips.

Though that is a vastly different darkness from the darkness of grief, there are perhaps elements in common—a sense of isolation, discouragement, uncertainty about the future.

What is to sustain us through the long periods of grief? What enables us not to be totally crushed?

Along with all kinds of help from our friends and our communities of faith, it is often a sense of the God within that helps us break from our darkness. A presence as gentle and insistent as the fragrance of flowers, as life-giving and warming as light.

I have a strength within myself that sometimes surprises me.

SEPTEMBER 1

> We can be a little more resistant to calls of duty, though
> responsibilities, too, can help us keep going. But if we
> tend to be superconscientious, we can relax a little . . .
> When we do go into social groups, we need not expect
> too much of ourselves or feel we have to be scintillating
> or muster up the small talk.
>
> —MARTHA WHITMORE HICKMAN

What we are suggesting is that we be kind to ourselves,
realizing we have sustained a major wound and need
time—maybe even a little self-indulgence—to recover.

If there is some level on which we feel responsible for
what has happened (even if it's only the "guilt of the survivor"), we may feel a need to work extra hard to prove
we deserve our place in life again.

Wrong! As the lapel button popular a few years ago
proclaimed, "I am a child of the universe. I have a right
to be here."

Or to quote the dying priest in *Diary of a Country Priest*,
"All is grace." Life is a gift none of us earns. We need to
take care of ourselves so we will be strong for another day.
Let someone else do the extra chores of life for a while.
We'll have our turn again, when we're feeling better.

*I need make no excuses to anyone—not even to myself—in tak-
ing time to let the depleted wells of my energy fill up again.*

What restraint or limit should there be to grief for one so dear?

—HORACE

There is no universal time frame for grieving. There are as many patterns as there are mourners. Much depends on what kind of support system we have and how able we are—often with the help of friends—to face and express our grief.

But one thing we don't need to be intimidated by is the implied or expressed opinions of self-appointed monitors who think we are grieving "too long," or "making too much fuss," or whatever admonition their words or presence sends us.

Of course, if we find ourselves totally nonfunctional after months have passed, we may want to seek professional help. But we can be sure a wise helper is *not* going to tell us we are grieving too long or too much. On the contrary, if we are stuck on the pathway to recovery, it's much more likely that we've not given ourselves permission to grieve openly and honestly enough.

So if someone says to us, by word or by action, "You should be over that by now," we can recall the words from the Talmud: "Judge no one before you have been in his place."

Only from within me can my timetable of grief be discovered.

September 3

> So I was long ago forgiven. I listened to my mother on her deathbed tell the doctor her son was "always a good boy," having forgiven me so deeply I thought it undercut her memory. It was more, it was profounder.
>
> —WILLIAM GIBSON

What are we to do with those nagging "if only" feelings that linger—If only I had (or hadn't) said that. If only I had gone to visit more often, or been less of a burden.

Have they forgiven us, those who have gone on before? We have only our conjectures. But if death is an experience of consciousness, then surely it is of enlarged consciousness, of more inclusive vision than we know here. "To know all is to forgive all," the saying goes.

Perhaps it is in anticipation of that enlarged consciousness, already drawing to itself those who are near death, that our loved ones forgive us with grace and compassion. And if they don't, if the occasion just doesn't present itself, we can forgive ourselves on their behalf, confident that they would have if they could.

All is forgiven. All is forgiven. All is forgiven.

There is a land of the living and a land of the dead and the bridge is love the only survival the only meaning.
—THORNTON WILDER

We know without being told that the bridge is love. We know that we have not stopped loving, and that wherever our loved one has gone, our love has followed.

And surely that love is reciprocated. Sometimes it seems almost palpably in the room with us. There are people who have had visions of their loved ones standing nearby, heard the sounds of their voices, even felt their intervention at a critical time.

A man who has written widely in the field of grief tells how he went to get on an airplane and it was as though a force field would not allow him through the door. After several attempts he walked back down the stairs and took another plane. The first plane subsequently crashed. Later, the image of his dead son came to his mind, saying, "Remember the time I wouldn't let you get on that plane?"

What is at work here, we do not know. We do know that love binds us to the dead and they to us—in stretchable, but not breakable bonds.

I know that love does not cease with the event of death.

SEPTEMBER 5

I sometimes hold it half a sin
To put in words the grief I feel;
For words, like nature, half reveal
And half conceal the Soul within.

—ALFRED TENNYSON

It's so hard to explain how we feel. When friends ask, and we sense that it's more than a routine polite inquiry, we want to tell them. Yet what to say?

The same anxiety besets those who try to express condolences. How many times have we heard people who've come from visiting a grieving friend lament, "I don't know whether I was any help at all. I didn't know what to say."

We know, since we've been on the receiving end of expressions of sympathy, that what is said is not as important as that the person has come to be with us, though it *is* possible to say "the wrong thing." We all have our contenders for a prize "wrong thing." A couple of mine are, "It's providential," and, "I'm so sorry your daughter has graduated to the higher consciousness"!

But with few exceptions, the expression of love and caring is what matters, not the words. In the same way, we who are groping to express our grief don't need to worry about accuracy or whether we're getting it all just right.

I can trust my feelings to help me speak the truth.

Who sees Me in all,
And sees all in Me,
For him I am not lost,
And he is not lost for Me.

—BHAGAVAD GITA

What we are grieved and sometimes terrified by is the sheer fact of loss. The loss of the loved one's presence, the loss of his or her love, the loss of his or her Being. How can we be content in a world from which our loved one is forever gone?

But the wisdom of this passage from the Bhagavad Gita, and of passages from other sacred Scriptures, is that the creation continues to embrace us and all those whom we love. We are still somehow bound together in a giant conspiracy of love, mutual care, and ongoing life. As we are not lost to creation, we are not lost to one another.

This is not to deny the pain of separation and the uncertainty of Not Knowing. "Faith," said the apostle Paul, "is the assurance of things hoped for, the conviction of things not seen." What we can be fairly sure of, from our own experience and from the experiences of others, is that there is more going on in the universe than we can detect with our five senses. "Now," Paul also said, "I see in a glass, darkly. Then I shall see face to face."

Creation holds us, one by one, and all together.

September 7

Snail, snail, glister me forward,
Bird, soft-sigh me home,
Worm, be with me.
This is my hard time.

—Theodore Roethke

Sometimes when we are sad, we have no interest in large-scale cosmic issues or in sweeping panoramas. Our affinities are with the small and intimate—the birds that flit through the trees, the snails and worms that live and work in the ground.

I don't know why these small creatures are a comfort to us, but they are. Perhaps it is their vulnerability, that they exist amidst the threats from larger elements—the vagaries of wind and water, the stomp of a foot or a shovel. We know what it is to feel small and struggling, and so do they. If they can go forth with resoluteness in the face of such odds against their survival—well, maybe we can, too.

For whatever reason, these lines from Roethke stayed with me through the darkest hours of my own loss, and even now I welcome the creatures—snail, bird, worm—as cohorts in the ongoing struggle and joy of life.

We are creatures, and we need one another.

I know that we live in the lives of those we touch. I have felt in me the living presence of many I have loved and who have loved me. I experience my daughter's presence with me daily. And I know that this is not limited to those we know in the flesh, for many guests of my life shared neither time nor space with me.

—ELIZABETH WATSON

All of us experience a kind of spiritual communion with friends who are not necessarily in our immediate physical presence. When we get together after long absences, it seems "as though it were yesterday." Is this perhaps partly because we do carry one another somewhere in our unconscious minds, though we are separated?

If with the living, why not with the dead? And this sense we have of knowing those whose words we read or whom we hear about, so that if they walked into the room we would know them—is this, too, evidence of a communion of spirits?

The world of the spirit is a world without walls—of time, of space, of physical reality. We can close our eyes, retreat into ourselves, and be at home with the throngs of people we know and love. Surely this is in some way akin to the "communion of saints" of which the mystics write.

When I am alone I can choose some company to be with me.

SEPTEMBER 9

On the wings of time Grief flies away.

—LA FONTAINE

There are many variations of this theme—that time is the great healer, that time heals all things.

Yes, and no. If one is able to process one's grief in a healthy, open way, then yes, time will certainly ease the pain. If one tries to bypass the grief, or is unable to work through its multiple strands in time may simply cover over grief, so that it never has a chance to heal. Then trouble will ensue—depression, fear of relationships, frenetic activity—who knows what?

And even if one proceeds through grief with the utmost wisdom, the figure of grief *flying* away seems a total exaggeration. Crawling, maybe? Or plodding?

How much time before one begins to really feel better depends on the nature of the loss—the age of the person, the closeness of the relationship, the circumstances of death. Grief groups, in which people have a common experience, can be a great help. They provide a safe place to grieve openly, and help evaluate in an accepting, non-threatening way whether their members are moving along or have somehow got stuck and need extra assistance.

Years from now, I may agree grief flies away in time. But don't push me.

As I write this it sounds rather negative and hard but I do not mean it to be so. Happiness grounded in reality is far deeper than that built upon fantasy, and suffering teaches one that happiness can catch a person unawares in the midst of deprivation and desolation. There is a certain stripping away of the externals which makes one more sensitive to joy as well as to sorrow.

—SHEILA CASSIDY

These words were written by a physician reflecting on her arrest and torture in Chile for treating a wounded revolutionary. The circumstances are different, but her experience of suffering as "stripping away of the externals" is akin to ours.

Then how gracious seem the small gifts that may come—a patch of sunlight on a cold floor, an unexpected gesture of friendship, the fragrant steam of hot tea.

Poet Mary Jane Irion recalls grieving all night over a death, and then

"in the terrible morning one of the neighbors brought doughnuts so good I never forgot them."

A sense of taste and texture—and gratitude for friendship—were only sharpened by grief.

◆◆

In the midst of darkness there is light; in the midst of sorrow, joy.

SEPTEMBER 11

Be still and listen to the stillness within.
—DARLENE LARSON JENKS

It is not enough just to be still.

Often in our moments of quiet our minds are scanning the horizon—not only the physical horizon, but the emotional horizon as well. And not only the present but the past. In our minds we run through past scenes when our loved one was present. We dwell on the occasions surrounding the loved one's death—how sad it was! How much we miss him or her! We may feel a hollowness within ourselves, now that the person has gone.

But there is another still place within us that is not hollow at all, because we are there. We are our own home, our own first occupant, and we have not gone away.

But if we are quiet and listen for our own stillness, how can we prevent all those other things from rushing in? We can't always. And that's fine. Sometimes we need to pay attention to those sad associations and memories, too.

But sometimes it's good to ask them to leave for a while, and to pay attention to our own *being*. One classical way of doing this is to breathe with great care and deliberation, and attend only to that. We may find this a good way to "ease into" our own stillness—a sense of our own body, mind, spirit, in this space, alone.

I have a place of peace within myself. I can find it.

I want, by understanding myself, to understand others. I want to be all that I am capable of becoming . . . This all sounds very strenuous and serious. But now that I have wrestled with it, it's no longer so. I feel happy—deep down. All is well.

—KATHERINE MANSFIELD

It is rough going—this passage through grief. It is a time of soul-searching. We are driven to examine ourselves, to look at what we have lost. What from the loved one stays with us? What do we hope to make of the rest of our lives?

So it is also a time of growth in understanding—of ourselves and of others. It is hard work, and it is done in sadness because we are sad.

But when the dust has settled, when the sharpest edges of the pain have eased, we will be wiser and more compassionate. We will be more self-assured because we have been through hard times and have prevailed. A security we hadn't known before may mark our life. We have looked death in the face and know that it is not all terror and confusion. As we learn to relinquish our loved one into the loving care of a Creator, we will feel a peace coming into our lives, a trust in the order of things, and a willingness to cherish one day at a time.

◆◆

Through this experience I will find in myself new strength and wisdom—perhaps, even, new joy.

SEPTEMBER 13

O! that this too too solid flesh would melt,
Thaw and resolve itself into a dew;
Or that the Everlasting had not fix'd
His canon 'gainst self-slaughter! O God! O God!
How weary, stale, flat, and unprofitable
Seem to me all the uses of this world.
—WILLIAM SHAKESPEARE

This is a state of depression with which we all are probably familiar. We would like to be removed from all
awareness. We may think about suicide. Nothing feels
good. Nothing tastes good. Nothing appeals to us. Nothing at all.

When this mood descends like a dark cloud, it is helpful
to remember that we have felt like this before, that others
have felt like this before—and that the mood will pass.

We can help move it away—though it may be hard to
muster energy for that—by doing something physically
demanding, like going for a strenuous walk, or for a swim.
Or by tending some plants. Or talking with a friend. Or
cooking. Anything to get us into a different frame of mind.

One friend suggested that at such times it was helpful
to her to repeat the phrase "The worst is over." It might
be worth a try.

*This cloud of darkness is understandable, given what I have been
through. But it will pass.*

Watch your way then, as a cautious traveller; and don't be gazing at that mountain or river in the distance, and saying, "How shall I ever get over them?" but keep to the present *little inch* that is before you, and accomplish *that* in the little moment that belongs to it. The mountain and the river can only be passed in the same way; and, when you come to them, you will come to the light and strength that belong to them.

—M. A. KELTY

A woman in her old age said that the only thing in her life she regretted was the time she had spent worrying.

Of course we look ahead in worry and regret. How shall we survive birthdays, family holidays, when we will so keenly miss our loved one?

These will be difficult times—and there will be others we don't anticipate. But we have no way of knowing what will befall us, or what would have befallen us—and our loved one—had he or she lived. Life is full of roads not taken, and while we mourn the expected companionship of a loved one—that, too, was never assured. So let's get off the worry-about-the-future track and savor the meaning of *this* day.

I will look upon this day as a gift, not to be squandered.

SEPTEMBER 15

Heaven will solve our problems, but not, I think, by showing us subtle reconciliations between all our apparently
contradictory notions. The notions will all be knocked
from under our feet. We shall see that there never was
any problem. And, more than once, that impression
which I can't describe except by saying that it's like the
sound of a chuckle in the darkness. The sense that some
shattering and disarming simplicity is the real answer.

—C. S. LEWIS

I suspect that a large part of the energy we spend in pondering the various possible scenarios of life after death is
just the energy of grief needing a place to go. But since
we are given to speculating—and since there is a persistent conviction found in many religions that there is life
beyond human death—perhaps we could throw our hats
into the ring of hope, and surmise that while we don't
know what God is doing in creation, God knows, and will
see us through.

*In attending to the mysteries of life and death, I will listen for
a chuckle in the darkness.*

But I am no more I,
Nor is my house now my house.
—FEDERICO GARCÍA LORCA

The death of a loved one shifts the whole foundation of our life. Nothing is as it was. Even what was most familiar seems in a strange way unfamiliar. It is as though we had to learn a new language, a new way of seeing. Even the face in the mirror sometimes seems the face of a stranger.

What are we to make of this? Just that we truly have, in a way, entered a new country. Though the terrain looks much the same and many of the people are the same people, there is a different light over everything.

Remember how long it took, when you moved to a new house or a new town, for it to seem like home? It is the same with any major life change. We will get used to this new land, this new arrangement of people and relationships. But it will take time—time to look around, to be startled, to be brought up short, again and again. An inner lurch of protest before we acknowledge—Oh, yes, it's different now.

I have entered a new country. Of course it feels strange.

SEPTEMBER 17

Take rest. The field that has rested gives a beautiful crop.
—OVID

One of the things we learn about grief is that it is exhausting. At first we may seem to have too much energy. We are "wired," going on nervous energy, often unable to sleep.

And then, sometimes in alternating waves of high energy and lassitude, we find our balance of rest and activity isn't working very well. We may be geared up for a week. Other times we seem to fall asleep at every opportunity— including times that could hardly be called opportune! And still we're tired.

What we need to realize is that our whole system has sustained a major shock, and it will take some time for our psyches and our bodies to adjust to the new alignments thrust upon them. This is labor of soul and body and it is draining.

We would do well to take care of ourselves, including getting extra rest.

Perhaps only when we "take rest" can we begin to see again the beauty of the world and recall in gratitude the legacy of the one we have lost.

I will care for myself in honor of my life and all who have shared that life with me.

An additional strain, connected with Fritz' long illness . . .
was my inability for two or three years to recall him as
he was before he got ill. I remember lying awake at
night, struggling in vain to recapture his image . . . How
much I suffered through this blockage I only realized fully
through the ecstasy of joy and relief when finally I could
again recall the younger, healthy Fritz.

—LILY PINCUS

When a loved one has died after a long illness—or enfee-
bled by advanced age, or after a disfiguring accident—it
is often hard to recover the full variety of images of that
person. We *know* the person didn't always look like that,
but that ill or disfigured face and body frequently crowd
out the vibrant images which have characterized our loved
one for most of our lives together.

Time will help us restore the balance. It may also be
helpful to look at photographs of happier, healthier times
and to remember the quality of those occasions. Those
early memories are not lost. They are clouded over for a
time, but they will step forward after a while to reclaim
their place.

The images of my loved one will return in their own time.

September 19

There is really no such creature as a single individual; he has no more life of his own than a cast-off cell marooned from the surface of your skin.

—Lewis Thomas

Somehow we know this. And we know it with special sharpness and poignancy when one who is close to us, as close as though he or she were a part of our own body, is taken away. Of course it hurts!

But there is some comfort, too, in this concept of being parts of one another's being. We are not alone in the world. We are bound to the rest of creation as cells in a body are bound together.

And not only bound to the living, but bound to the dead. We feel this to be true as well, though we don't understand how.

So what else is new? Perhaps we can just rest in our ignorance, savoring what we share with all life, buoyed by the knowledge of how totally *unalone* we are.

I am organically connected to all of life. I am not alone!

The main impact is just the loss, the incredible loss. The expectations just were gone. The old age that I expected is different. It just never occurred to me that she would not be in the next rocker . . . At the Catholic school that I went to, the motto was *hic et noc,* Latin for "here and now." What they meant was you do what is necessary—here and now.

—COKIE ROBERTS

Cokie Roberts was commenting on the death of her sister.

All of us who have suffered the untimely death of a loved one could echo her words. We have to begin again to learn about our own growing old.

But the real lesson of untimely death—or of any death—is, Pay attention to today. "Do what is necessary—here and now." The compliment you mean to give, the time together you keep putting off, the resolution of an old pain you yearn to talk about but haven't got around to—these are the things to attend to, before it is too late.

If it's too late to talk to one already gone, then play through in your imagination both sides of the conversation you never had. You may be surprised at how healing this exercise can be. And then find the people for whom it's not too late, and tell them what you want them to know.

This is the only day I have for sure. May I use it well.

SEPTEMBER 21

I don't believe you dead. How can you be dead if I still feel you? Maybe, like God, you changed into something different that I'll have to speak to in a different way, but you not dead to me Nettie. And never will be. Sometimes when I get tired of talking to myself I talk to you.

—ALICE WALKER

It *is* hard to believe—that a loved one has died.

And for a while we do feel his or her presence. This may be more than our own projection. People tell of being aware of just when the spirit of the dead takes leave of a room, of silent exchanges, of visitations that follow soon after the death of a loved one.

Whether these are real or imagined, we certainly continue to *think* toward the dead, to carry on imagined conversations with them. One mourner told of how healing it was for him to go often to the cemetery and talk to his departed love.

It is a favored therapy, too, in healing unresolved hurts and misunderstandings. "What would you say to her?" "What do you imagine she might say back to you?"

Sometimes the veil between the living and the dead seems thin, and lighter than air.

Exhaust the little moment. Soon it dies.
And be it gash or gold it will not come
Again in this identical disguise.
—GWENDOLYN BROOKS

For a while we are so infused with grief over our loss that we can think of little else. Everything else seems an intrusion. If people call us on other matters, we think, *Don't you know there isn't space in my life for that right now?*

But grieving can be habit-forming, and after a while we need to move on. Retreat into our own small world and its painful security will not protect us from further dangers. But it may keep us from savoring the world—its beauties and relationships, which are also passing, and which our loved one would want us to enjoy to the full.

My small son once endeared himself to me by saying, as he stood at the doorway of my room, where I was, atypically, still in bed, "How can I have any fun downstairs when I know you're up here with the flu?" Gratifying, but I wouldn't have wanted him to spend the morning moping around—and I'm sure he didn't!

As I am able, I will reenter the world around me with courage and expectation.

SEPTEMBER 23

Great peace is found in little busy-ness.

—CHAUCER

Such a monumental event has occurred. Our response to it is so total; we are devastated.

What can we do, faced as we are with this tidal wave of feeling and change?

Nothing big. Nothing monumental.

At first we will do what is required of us: make arrangements, plan services, greet our friends, think about food and lodging for people who may have come from out of town.

But when all that is over—then what?

First, rest. And then, find things to do.

It will be no problem, finding things to do. The effort will be doing them. They may seem futile—why sew on a button when my world has fallen apart? Why rake the leaves when the future looks bleak and I don't care about the lawn?

But as we begin to busy ourselves—in small, productive tasks—we will find some of our free-floating confusion and sorrow being absorbed, like water into a sponge, into the task we are performing. We will begin to think in terms of what we might want to do next, maybe even make some new plans for the future. Our hearts will grow lighter; our steps will quicken. A yes to life, after all.

Today I will do one "optional" thing.

When my father was an old man, he surprised me by remarking that he understood what my mother's death meant to me but had no idea what to do about it. I think it would have been something if he had just said this.
—WILLIAM MAXWELL

One of the delicate issues within a family that has lost a loved one is how much and what to say to one another.

Perhaps it will help if we can talk about the process— "Do you feel like talking now, or would you rather be left alone?" "I'd like to talk about _____, but if you'd rather not now—or ever—that's okay." We need to be as sure as we can that we are not misinterpreting one another's signals, and often there's no way to find that out without asking.

Particularly with children, we may refrain from acknowledging their grief and ours in some effort to protect them. They need our sharing, not our silence. What is unspoken is often more fearful than shared pain. Children are no strangers to tears and puzzlement. They need us, as we need them.

It is probably better to risk saying too much than to hold back out of fear.

SEPTEMBER 25

> It was coming to John that when the great people in one's life die, one is forced to be more oneself. One is forced to grow up.
>
> —MAY SARTON

A young woman mourning the death of her father said that when she accepted that death was all right, she found within herself a whole new well of energy from which to draw in developing her own life.

We may resist such a notion. To ascribe any "benefits" to our loss might imply a diminishment not only of our own sense of loss, but also of the importance of the person we love. If we can get along well without him or her, does it mean the person wasn't as crucial to our life as we had thought?

Not at all. The new energy available to us was formed and nourished in the richness of our relationship with that person. The self that we are will carry our loved one's imprint forever. We have not abandoned him or her any more than he or she has abandoned us. If we find in ourselves a new maturity, that is part of the person's legacy to us, and he or she would wish us godspeed. But we must be willing to let it happen.

I will carry with me forever the strength my loved one bequeathed to me.

The pattern has shifted . . . I am no longer anybody's child. I have become the Grandmother . . .

The rhythm of the fugue alters; the themes cross and recross. The melody seems unfamiliar to me, but I will learn it.

—MADELEINE L'ENGLE

The whole system of our lives is disturbed by loss. We have to learn new patterns—as a flooded river when it retreats leaves behind a new configuration of tributaries.

It will take us a while to get used to all this. At times we may forget and begin to respond the way we did. How many tickets for the play? How many places at the table? How many fresh towels for the bathroom? Small matters, but quickening reminders.

The more profound shifts of who we are in the world will last a lot longer. If we have lost a parent, we have lost part of our buffer against being the "older generation," with all that implies. If we have lost a child, a whole future together is wiped away. If a sibling, one of the sharers of our early years is gone.

Though it may be heavy going for a while, we will re-align our patterns of thought and expectation so we can be grateful for the life—and the memories—that we have.

Though the waters of change swirl around me, still I am safe.

September 27

To keep a lamp burning we have to keep putting oil in it.

—Mother Teresa

At first we are almost immobilized. We do what we have to do and are grateful for the customs and rituals that guide us through those first days. There are many to care for us—other loved ones, friends, members of our community of faith.

But then that wave of support recedes and we must learn to assume care of ourselves.

How to do that? We may cultivate new interests. Do we have a talent for painting? For music? Artistic ventures are wonderful ways to lose oneself in work—and also, often, to express one's grief. Some people seek out grief recovery groups, in which you can share what is in your heart without wondering whether you're imposing on friends who may not understand your need to tell your story again and again. Some join service networks like Foster Grandparents or Alive Hospice, which helps the dying and their families.

The important thing is that, like a lamp that needs oil, we, too, need to keep our sources of healing and energy fed.

I have the power—and responsibility—to keep my life moving.

For now we see in a mirror, dimly, but then we will see face to face. Now I know only in part; then I will know fully, even as I have been fully known. And now faith, hope, and love abide, these three; and the greatest of these is love.

—I CORINTHIANS 13:12-13

How we long to be known to one another

Or do we? For many of us there persists the suspicion: if you really knew me, you wouldn't like me. But in therapy groups and sharing groups across the land comes the astonishing discovery: to really know me *is* to love me. Not because I am perfect—far from it—but because in sharing my vulnerability and pain and weakness, I become understood and accepted. In the strength of that gift, I can grow and change. Like newly tilled earth, I am ready for fresh seeds, for new growth.

The "now" and "then" in the passage from Paul's letter to the church at Corinth describe the clouded and imperfect knowledge and love we experience in life, and the state of full enlightenment and love we will know on the other side of death.

◆◆

When burdened with feelings of self-doubt and anxiety about unresolved conflict, I will try to imagine a truly forgiving world.

SEPTEMBER 29

Haste, haste, has no blessing.

—SWAHILI PROVERB

At first we are so busy—so much to do, people to talk with, arrangements to make.

Then come the quiet times, and in some ways they are harder to bear. Our loneliness stares out at us from the mirror. All the places we used to go to together, we go to alone. Even if we go with someone else, the gap is still there.

In defense, we may start to hurry about, hoping that by keeping ourselves so busy, maybe we won't notice how much it hurts.

It's good to be active, of course. We do need other people, and activities in which to involve ourselves. But don't make the mistake of doing this to hide from grief. It will find us in the end and demand its hearing.

To inhabit the province of grief for a while is, oddly enough, its own comfort. It is, for a period, our home; it is where we belong, and we need to rest there in quiet and at leisure until we understand its spaces and its meaning. Then we can move on.

Without hurry or panic I will dwell in the house of my grief.

All that we do
Is touched with ocean, yet we remain
On the shore of what we know.

—Richard Wilbur

We who stand close to the mystery of death yearn to know more. What is it like to make that crossing? *Is* it a crossing, or is this the end? In the power of faith and hope, we believe that our loved ones have gone on to greater glory.

But what is that like? The old images of palaces and golden streets don't work for us anymore. What, then? Do the dead know our lives? Do they know how we love and miss them? People who report near-death experiences tell of hovering above their bodies watching efforts to resuscitate them—and report moving toward images of light and love so inviting that it is almost difficult to come back. And when they—or any of us—die, do our spirits stay around for a while and then move on? Do our loved ones come to meet us when we go?

We can't know the answers to these questions, but we play with them from time to time, and trust that we will learn what we need to know when we need to know it. So we stand at the edges, and wonder.

◆◆

I trust that what is unknown to me is for my good and my ultimate peace and joy.

OCTOBER 1

They that sow in tears shall reap in joy. He that goeth forth and weepeth, bearing precious seed, shall doubtless come again with rejoicing, bringing his sheaves with him.

—PSALM 126

This reference in the Bible is for a people far from home, anticipating their return. It can also be a metaphor for following the grief process courageously, confident that after a season of winnowing and growing, we will come back to our state of equilibrium, even joy, enriched and made strong and productive by our difficult passage through grief. Had we not ventured forth into this strange and new terrain—had we stayed back, unwilling to move—we would not return in joy with the riches of our difficult passage. We carry these riches not only for ourselves, but for others who will need our help as they in turn venture into their own journeys of recovery.

May we be brave to set forth, brave to continue when we reach lands that are new and strange to us, brave to trust those who are there to help us, brave and compassionate as we return to help others.

I will set forth on this journey in hope and trust. What more have I to lose? And how much to gain!

All I know from my own experience is that the more loss we feel the more grateful we should be for whatever it was we had to lose. It means we had something worth grieving for. The ones I'm sorry for are the ones that go through life not even knowing what grief is.

—FRANK O'CONNOR

This is cold comfort just now—the thought that we should be grateful we're not like those poor unfortunates who have never loved anyone this much. Consumed as we are by our grief, we cannot imagine being in such a situation. Perhaps we are a little indignant, too—it's supposed to make us feel better that there are people infinitely worse off than we?

But we do know we wouldn't trade with them—wouldn't trade the years we've enjoyed the presence of our loved one for freedom from pain—at the cost of never having known this loved person at all. No, that's not a bargain we ever wanted to strike. What we want is to have our loved one back, in health and safety.

But since that's not possible, maybe it would temper our grief a little to acknowledge how blessed we are to have had a love that rich. Though the person has gone, the gift that that love has been goes on and on and on.

◆◆

Saddened as I am by loss, my heart lifts in gratitude for the richness _____ has brought to my life.

OCTOBER 3

As the months pass and the seasons change, something of tranquillity descends, and although the well-remembered footstep will not sound again, nor the voice call from the room beyond, there seems to be about one in the air an atmosphere of love, a living presence . . . It is as though one shared, in some indefinable manner, the freedom and the peace, even at times the joy, of another world where there is no more pain . . . The feeling is simply there, pervading all thought, all action. When Christ the healer said, "Blessed are they that mourn, for they shall be comforted," he must have meant just this.

—DAPHNE DU MAURIER

There are stages and stages of grieving and they come and go, inconstant. But after a while, even though the dips and swells continue to appear, there seems to seep into the life of the griever a confidence, hard-won, that underlies all the swirls and tides of life's ongoing struggles and joys. A sense that we have hit rock bottom and come slowly back, and that, though we will have further trials and doubts (and we will!), there is a level of stability and confidence which, even in dark hours, we will know is there and will not let us drop through the bottom of the sea.

The eternal God is thy refuge and underneath are the everlasting arms.—Deuteronomy 33:27

> Great Spirit, now I pray to you . . .
> Great Spirit, hear me;
> My soul is weary,
> Now I pray that your spirit will dwell in me.
>
> —KIOWA PRAYER

Sometimes we are so tired. Grief is tiring. Our sorrow saps our strength and resolve, and the one for whom we grieve—who was often a source of energy and strength to us—is gone. So we mourn our loss—and who is there to help us?

There are many to help us—friends, other family members, whatever communities of support we are a part of. Still, a pervasive sense of fatigue, and even despair, can seem our constant companion.

Now is the time to risk believing. The time to risk believing that there is, in the structure of the universe, a Spirit that waits, in longing and welcome, for us to turn and say, "Come to me. Fill me with your presence. I cannot handle this by myself. Help me. Be my energy, and my rest." We may be surprised at the lift this gives us, an easing of our burden, a sense that we are not alone.

Spirit, whoever you are, wherever you are, be with me now.

OCTOBER 5

I sit on the rich, moist earth, green earth, and draw my knees to my chest. All is not lost. The birds have simply moved on. They give me the courage to do the same.
—TERRY TEMPEST WILLIAMS

At this time of year in some parts of our country, we begin to see the birds fly south for a long season. How do they know? How will they know to come back?

The answers are out of our hands. The processes of life go on, irrespective of our knowledge or ignorance. How reassuring that we don't *need* to know, that the Creator who set the globes of the solar system spinning does know. And the birds do come back.

Can we extend the same trust to our experiences of loss and renewal? Can we watch birds go, secure in the expectation of their return?

Can we say goodbye to our loved ones—not in the expectation that they will come flying back in the spring, but that, in ways we cannot know, they will continue to be present to us, continue to love us, as we continue to love them?

In the turning of the seasons, I find promise and hope.

When she came through the door of the children's room she could feel his presence as strongly throughout the room as if she had opened a furnace door; the presence of his strength, of virility, of helplessness, and of pure calm.

—JAMES AGEE

People have described in many ways this sense of a transformed presence at the time of or soon after death. For some it is just that—a sense of presence. Others report a conversation in which the one who has died asks reassurance that it's all right to go. Still others tell of observing on the face of the dying person, and perhaps in some final utterances, what appears to be a reunion with loved ones who have gone before.

What are we to make of these experiences? Surely they have profound and personal meanings to those present. But even for those of us who only hear about them, they are at the very least a hint that life moves on from death, and they offer hope that we shall be with our loved ones again.

Before the mystery of death, let us stand with open hearts and minds.

> She never told her love,
> But let concealment, like a worm i' the bud,
> Feed on her damask cheek: she pin'd in thought,
> And with a green and yellow melancholy,
> She sat like Patience on a monument,
> Smiling at grief.
>
> —WILLIAM SHAKESPEARE

The picture here, from *Twelfth Night*, is of a woman who assumed a mask of calm tranquility, while inside, "like a worm i' the bud," the feelings were eating away. She smiled through her grief—and was likened to stone.

Let it be a lesson to us! Holding tight to our feelings, trying to keep a stiff upper lip, may present a soothing image to the world. But at what cost? The cost of growing numb?

And for whose protection? Our own—that we not be considered "too emotional"? That we be regarded as pillars of stability and faith? For the protection of others, so they don't have to see how sad losing a loved one can make you feel?

They know better, and so do we. And our closeness is enhanced by sharing our grief, much more so than by the misguided attempt to keep it all under control.

I will not take on a facade of false calm—and turn to stone.

We have only to believe. And the more threatening and irreducible reality appears, the more firmly and desperately must we believe. Then, little by little, we shall see the universal horror unbend, and then smile upon us, and then take us in its more than human arms.

—TEILHARD DE CHARDIN

How we long to believe in a Creator who loves and guides us, who holds us—and our loved one—in continuing life and possibility! It is almost too good to be true.

Do we turn away from belief because we don't want to fool ourselves with false hope? Are we afraid of believing because we might be wrong?

Think of all the scientific truths that would never have been discovered had someone not risked that a hypothesis arrived at by intuition and speculation was worth experimenting with.

But how to test the hypothesis of belief? In our sadness and despair, can we act and think as though faith is an accurate mirror of truth; that there is, out there in the darkness, a hand that reaches out to us in compassion and love?

It's worth a try.

I will take the risk of believing and see where it leads me.

OCTOBER 9

. . . the dead have an afterlife in the form of a continuing
influence on their survivors. This seems to be particularly
true when they leave us with unresolved feelings of anger
or guilt. The living may feel relief when death ends pa-
rental demands on our energies or a long and painful
illness. If part of the process of bereavement is a search
for the beloved, we also allow the dead to seek us out,
until gradually we come to terms with their claims and
ask them to let us be.

—MARY JANE MOFFAT

The psychic drama that follows the loss of loved ones has
infinite variations.

Is there a way in which we're relieved? They may have
been a great care to us, a sap on our physical and emotional energy. Or perhaps they made life difficult in other
ways, creating all kinds of stress in the family. Is it okay
to acknowledge that in some ways it's easier without
them?

What if, in our minds, they look at us reproachfully—
How could you? You know it was partly your fault.

So we have a lengthy go-around in our minds, seeking
a perfect resolution—which will not come. Until, wearying
of the fray and counting on the grace of mutual forgiveness, perhaps we can Let It Go.

Let us accept each other, knowing we did the best we could.

In our sleep, pain which cannot forget falls drop by drop
upon the heart until, in our own despair, against our will,
comes wisdom through the awful grace of God.
—AESCHYLUS

Grief engulfs us, takes over our lives, renders us impotent.
What are we to do?

Wait. Get through one day. Then another. And another.

We will feel as though we are only "going through the
motions," but it is important to go through the motions.

We are, in a strange way, relearning that we are alive.

We are alive, functioning, and can do what we need to
do. But just barely.

Then one day we're surprised (because how could it be
so?) to realize that some of our energy has come back.

How did it happen? We didn't expect it, didn't even
particularly want it to happen, because we had no expectation of *anything* happening. The important thing had already passed—the loss of our loved one.

But there it is. And our step lightens. And we begin to
look around.

For all evidence of life where I felt only death, let me be grateful.

OCTOBER 11

He who cannot forgive others breaks the bridge over which he must pass himself.

—GEORGE HERBERT

Sometimes we have suffered terrible injustice at the hands of those who have died. If our whole experience with such a person has been bad, we may need resolution from other kinds of feelings, but sadness may not be first on the list!

Now the person has gone. We are left with unfinished business in our hands and we don't know what to do.

We may need professional help—a counselor or therapist who will guide us through this swamp of ambivalence, or maybe just a friend to talk with. We, too, are not perfect, but that doesn't make us unworthy, unlovable, or unloved.

But, more for our own sake than for the reputation of the one who has died, it is essential that, to the extent we are able, we forgive the wrongs done to us.

A word of caution: to forgive is not to gloss over or to excuse. If there have been real wounds, they need real attention. Chances are we will know from the relief we feel, the lifting of a burden, when that forgiveness and reconciliation have occurred.

To forgive is to be freed of a burden.

OCTOBER 12

Incredibly, I've gone all afternoon without thinking of her.
—HOYT HICKMAN

We thought we would never be able to do it—move back into the active stream of the life we had known before this loss occurred.

And, of course, it's not the same life. Not only is the cast of characters diminished by one, but we, having been affected by this loss, are not the same person we were. And, depending on how close other key people in our life were to the one who is gone, perhaps neither are they.

But one day we realize we are beginning to come into our new life—where we are not always weighted down by grief. We may find ourselves enjoying a dish of ice cream or a cup of hot tea without reference to what is missing from our lives. We may watch a movie or a play without the complication of being a viewer for whom everything is colored by grief. We may finish a conversation with a friend and realize that not once did our loss seem to lie like an undertow beneath that exchange. Then we know we have moved onto a new path in our healing journey.

I know I cannot force it, but, bit by bit, recovery will come.

October 13

Come to me, come to me, O my God;
  Come to me everywhere!
Let the trees mean thee, and the grassy sod,
  And the water and the air!

—George Macdonald

When we have lost a loved one, we are hungry for assurance that God exists and holds the world in tender care. We need to know that life itself is not rejecting us, turning from our pain. Our antennae are out for signals, for signs and wonders—any hint that life cares for us, that God cares for us, that we are not alone.

We see significance in everything. A bird hovers by our window and seems to be singing to us. We run into someone we hadn't seen for a long time who, upon hearing of our loss, tells a wonderfully reassuring story of life after death. We go to church or synagogue and the service seems especially attuned to our need just then.

How much of this is our projection, how much the synergy of benign forces beyond our understanding, we don't know.

And maybe we don't need to know. Whatever its origin, something is coming to our aid. Perhaps God in many forms.

Sometimes I have a sense that life is calling my name, bringing me comfort.

To read the works of others who have gone through grief is another way of keeping the process going, and of finding another understanding friend. When a writer describes for me how I am feeling, she or he becomes my friend; I am not alone. Somehow that person has achieved some peace with the pain, enough to write it down. Maybe I, too, will find my way through this.
—MARTHA WHITMORE HICKMAN

In the crisis of losing a loved one, as in most other crises in life, we can be helped most by those who have been through the same thing.

In addition to friends who may have had experiences like ours, and to community support groups for grievers, don't overlook libraries and bookstores! There are books tailored to particular types of loss—of a parent, a spouse, a child. Some tell personal stories; some are more from the point of view of a counselor, offering clinical analysis and help. Some are from a particular religious or philosophical point of view.

In a bookstore or library we can browse until we find something that speaks to us. Variety isn't what matters here. It's like good friends—one or two may be all we need.

◆◆

The discovery of the right book can bring hope and wisdom, be a companion in the dark watches of the night.

OCTOBER 15

Because of her, he had learned to look for the birds—
the darting flight of wild canaries (yellow sun on yellow
wings), the chesty preening of redbirds and bluebirds, the
blackbird with the red-tipped wings like startling epaulets.
　　　　　　　　　　　　　　　　　　　—TERRY KAY

How much we have learned from them—those dear ones
we have lost! And how their gifts stay with us.

The sharp vignettes surface from our memory again and
again. Scenes we scarcely gave a second thought to when
our loved one was alive emerge as scenes from a family
album—doubly cherished now that our loved one is gone.

I see my mother cutting long, thin triangles from a
brightly colored page from a magazine, spreading them
with flour paste and, starting at the wide end, rolling these
strips around a needle—another bead for the necklaces she
was making for her two young daughters. I've never seen
this craft described (some kind of forerunner of papier-
mâché, I suppose) and I have no idea what became of the
necklaces. It was decades ago, and I don't know that I
thought of it again while she was alive. But I think of it
now with warmth and gratitude—my sister and I and our
mother, gathered around the table in this project of scis-
sors and paste and those wondrous beads!

*Our loved ones live on in the vivid memories of the things they
taught us.*

Excessive mourning is nonproductive, someone remarks. A social inconvenience, downright inconsiderate in the public eye. Life, according to my Orientalist friend, is a passage, a corridor, and she bids me to rid myself of morbid brooding.

Bullshit! I'm angry.

—TOBY TALBOT

No one wants to be inconsiderate of others, but right now it's more important that we not be inconsiderate of ourselves. We have been wounded. We need care. We need care from others, and we need care from ourselves. No one but we ourselves can know which is the best way to express our grief. And if we're angry—and it's legitimate to be angry at this blow that has been dealt us—we need to express our anger.

So if we make other people uncomfortable, or if we seem to be "more upset" than they think we should be—that's their problem. It's time for us to move on to other friends who are more understanding.

I will not be intimidated by the opinions of others on how I should be feeling. I am inside my head and heart, and I know.

OCTOBER 17

Make me to say, when all my griefs are gone,
"Happy the heart that sighed for such a one!"
—SAMUEL DANIEL

If we didn't love them, we wouldn't care so much.

At first the grief is so consuming, it may be hard to look ahead and foresee rejoicing—that we have been privileged to share life with this person.

Even when death is premature and the circumstances are terrible, we can know that, down the road, our gratitude for the life of the person will far outstrip the terrible grief that at first seems to take up the whole landscape of our lives. A friend whose son committed suicide told me that an important milestone in her healing was the making of two lists: one, of the bad things about her experience with this son; and another, of the good things. Needless to say, the list of good things was by far the longer list.

It will take time before the scale, tipped initially with the primary weight of grief, rebalances itself and our joy in the person's life again takes preeminence. But if the relationship has been one of joy and mutual appreciation, this will happen.

I am grateful, from the bottom of my heart, that I have shared the life of my loved one. And I trust that someday my happiness, as I remember our life together, will far outweigh the grief I feel now.

'Twant me, 'twas the Lord. I always told him, "I trust to you. I don't know where to go or what to do, but I expect you to lead me," and he always did.

—HARRIET TUBMAN

How do people get through adversity?

To Harriet Tubman, a fugitive black woman who, though there was a price on her head, returned to the South nineteen times to help move slaves to freedom on the underground railroad, it was her trust in God that saw her through.

She didn't know, any more than we do, "where to go or what to do," but she trusted the power that had sustained her and given her courage to prevail against the recurrent crises in her life.

We each have our own ways, our own traditions, for meeting the terrors of uncertain futures, the undulating waves of grief. It is helpful if, in our grief, we can stretch out our hand into the darkness and imagine the One who is reaching toward us to offer us comfort, and direction, and assurance of life to come.

O God, your sea is so great and my boat is so small. Be with me.

OCTOBER 19

. . . how complicated and individual mending is; the time required for healing cannot be measured against any fixed calendar.

—MARY JANE MOFFAT

All kinds of factors go into the matter of how long it takes to pass through the heaviest stages of grief. The end of the first year is an important milestone: one has then passed every anniversary, every special holiday.

But some have suggested that that is just the beginning: now the fact has sunk in, occasion by occasion, and there is still the rest of one's life to live.

Four years after my daughter's death, I realized one day, "This is beginning to feel different." Not that intense grief had left, but it was no longer such a preoccupying burden, the dominant fact of each day. Another writer says it takes seven years to recover from the death of someone close.

These are discouraging numbers to contemplate when one is first plunged into grief and a week looms ahead full of sadness. Time extends itself, stretches.

That will not always be the case. But there's no predicting. We must feel our way along, trusting the process to reveal its own wisdom.

I live one day at a time.

More than anything I have learned that we are all frail people, vulnerable and wounded; it is just that some of us are more clever at concealing it than others! And of course the great joke is that it is O.K. to be frail and wounded because that is the way the almighty transcendent God made people.

—SHEILA CASSIDY

What is this myth about being strong? About "keeping a stiff upper lip"? Of course, if we could choose, we'd like to do our weeping in a place where we won't cast a pall of gloom over some bright social occasion.

But who was ever ostracized for giving way to tears? If you have to explain, explain. If people are impatient—that's their problem. You have enough to contend with in your life right now without the extra burden of worrying about whether other people are going to be uncomfortable. If they've had a similar experience in their lives, they'll know right away what's going on. If they haven't—yet—maybe when sorrow comes their way, they'll be grateful for the permission to grieve that your tears have given them. You are not a stranger, acting strangely. You are a human being, acting like a human being.

◆◆

In the map of the created world, the path to healing does not skirt around the edges of grief but goes right through the middle.

If you wish me to weep, you yourself
Must first feel grief.

—HORACE

Why is it easier to express our grief in the presence of some people rather than others?

We don't need our friends to weep with us (though sometimes they do), but we do need to experience their empathy, their understanding, in order to feel we have permission to grieve openly in their presence.

It isn't so much a matter of specific words that give us permission as it is whether we believe they are fully present to us, that their minds aren't half off on some other subjects. If we are going to be vulnerable enough to express our grief to them, we want their full attention.

But not simply their full attention. We want them to be nonjudgmental and sympathetic.

We want a lot. But we are giving a lot, too, in sharing our deepest selves with them. And like the tender shoots when a plant is most vulnerable, our feelings of grief and sadness—and the trust to share those—are easily bruised.

We experience this now as a griever. It will stand us in good stead when it is our turn to be the consoling friend.

Knowing how much I need sensitive listening will surely help me be a sensitive listener for others.

Trouble not thyself by pondering life in its entirety . . .
Rather, as each occasion arises in the present, put this
question to thyself: "Where lies the unbearable, unendurable part of this task?" . . . Next recall to mind that
neither past nor future can weigh thee down, only the
present. And the present will shrink to littleness if thou but
set it apart, assign it its boundaries, and then ask thy mind
if it avail not to bear even this!

—MARCUS AURELIUS

The sorrow of the moment is often difficult enough for us
to deal with. But when we let ourselves brood about past
events or think of the future times when we shall miss our
loved one so sharply, then we are in real trouble! The
past—as we know only too well—is over. The future is
unknowable. Each day we encounter forks in the road, and
always leave behind us alternatives we did not choose. The
same will be the case in the future—it is a maze whose
patterns we cannot know.

So, as much as we are able, let's limit our concern to
this day only. Chances are that on most days we'll be able
to handle things quite well!

*My experience of today is its own journey and I will savor it
for what it is.*

OCTOBER 23

"Why not" is a slogan for an interesting life.
—MASON COOLEY

At first our energy is absorbed in doing the necessary things—making arrangements, speaking with those who come to console us. After the immediate hubbub is over, we are probably exhausted. Then, when some strength to do "optional things" begins to come back, we probably return to our conventional patterns and activities, glad for the security of "the usual."

But our life has changed now, with the event of this loss. Perhaps it is time to take the energy we poured into that relationship (and often there was a lot of physical care) and turn to some new thing. Think of it. Let your imagination wander; poke around in the attic of your mind, where you've stashed away some dreams. What New Thing might you want to try?

Do you dare? Why not? Think of your loved one as blessing your effort, smiling through the veil that separates life from death, cheering you on—"Go ahead. Give it a try. I dare you. You know I'd love to have you succeed. And you may. This is the time!"

I will appropriate my loved one's courage, and blessing, and dare a New Thing.

When it seems that our sorrow is too great to be borne, let us think of the great family of the heavy-hearted into which our grief has given us entrance, and inevitably, we will feel about us their arms, their sympathy, their understanding.

—HELEN KELLER

Remember how it is when you meet someone who has had a loss similar to yours? The instant bond, the acknowledgment in the other's face—*I know you. I know what you're going through.* And your own feeling, which is almost a physical lightening of the burden, that here is someone who understands.

You will meet such kindred souls, perhaps more often than you expect. People will refer them to you—"I think it would be helpful if you talked with _____." You will probably run into fellow mourners in groups to which you belong, as though by some principle of natural selection you gravitate toward one another.

And there will be fellow sufferers whom you may never meet but whose sorrow you may read about or hear of. Your heart will go out to them, and the well of human compassion on which we all draw will be deepened.

In my mind I reach out to fellow sufferers—met and unmet—and feel our support for one another.

OCTOBER 25

O Lord, my heart is not lifted up,
  my eyes are not raised too high;
I do not occupy myself with things too great and too
  marvelous for me.
But I have calmed and quieted my soul,
  like a child quieted at its mother's breast;
  like a child that is quieted is my soul.

—PSALM 131

Our mind flies this way and that, speculating about destiny and truth, the state of our loved one, what we can believe, and how we shall manage all that lies ahead. These are questions without answers. Yet we continue to worry, like a dog worrying a bone.

There are places and times when we need to think about all these things. But we also need to give ourselves some respite, realize that we are not responsible for the fate of even our private world, let alone for answering cosmic questions.

Think of an infant—helpless, knowing so little, sometimes so agitated—and how at its mother's breast that infant becomes a picture of contentment and peace. The image from the Psalmist is good for us to remember when life seems too much and we don't know where to turn.

Like a child that is quieted is my soul.

Grace strikes us when we are in great pain and restlessness . . . Sometimes at that moment a wave of light breaks into our darkness, and it is as though a voice were saying, "You are accepted."

—PAUL TILLICH

How we berate ourselves. Why aren't we able to look beyond this? Why aren't we better grievers? If we are people of faith, why aren't we able to let the faith we profess sustain us?

There's more. What about those times we snapped at our loved one, or weren't sensitive to his or her questions and state of mind, or went somewhere else when we knew that person would relish a visit from us? And on and on.

Would our loved one want us to feel all this extra anguish in addition to the sorrow of our loss? Was our loved one perfect? Is anyone?

No more are we. And don't have to be. No one else expects that of us, nor do we of others.

Most of us do the best we can. So let's walk out of the brooding darkness of self-condemnation, take a deep breath, turn toward the light of love which embraces us all, and hear those words—"Let go of all that. 'You are accepted.' "

For this moment, at least, I will let go of all those questions about my self-worth and know that I am acceptable just as I am.

OCTOBER 27

My grief and pain are mine. I have earned them. They are part of me. Only in feeling them do I open myself to the lessons they can teach.

—ANNE WILSON SCHAEF

When our whole sense of ourselves seems wounded and vulnerable, one of the ways we can claim our rightful presence in the world is to claim the legitimacy of our grief. That is who we are right now, and it is a valid way to be. We cannot escape the reality of ourselves as grieving persons any more than we can escape the reality of the death of the loved one.

In time we will see ourselves again in broader terms. But if, for a while, grieving is the main aspect of our being, then so be it. We may well move away from it sooner if we embrace that reality now. We don't owe anyone else an apology. We don't owe ourselves one, either.

Only by living my grief fully will I be able to walk through it and learn what it has to tell me.

Shall we live in mystery and yet conduct ourselves as though everything were known?

—CHRISTOPHER FRY

When we are grieving, everything has significance. We see meanings in what appear to be random events and wonder what is going on. A flower blooms in our garden out of season. The phone rings when we are feeling desolate and lonely, and it is a friend: "I was sitting here reading and I had a sudden urge to call you." A bird lands on a tree branch outside our window and bobs up and down, chirping and singing, for a very long time.

Are these all just coincidences? Is it possible that in the mysteries of creation, the Powers, God, the energies that move the world—even our departed loved one—are looking out for us? We would like to think so. And when we get together with others who have been through grief, we share our stories—shyly at first—and our skin tingles and our hearts are made glad and we think, Yes, it might be so.

There is always room for doubt. There is also room for faith and hope. That is the nature of mystery.

I will accept as gifts all intimations of love and care.

OCTOBER 29

Be still, my heart, these great trees are prayers.
—RABINDRANATH TAGORE

When we are grieving, we're apt to feel in some ways alone, cut off from other people and other living things.

It is salutary to go outside and stand by a tree. To stand in the presence of a great tree is to feel a kind of solidarity with nature, a continuity between oneself and the whole created world.

Now move closer, and put the palms of your hands against the bark of the tree. Feel the bark with your fingers. Think of the tree's age—how long it has been here, through summer and winter; how it draws its energy up from the earth and down from sunshine and rain.

Then stand closer yet, lean against the tree, and put your arms around it (hoping the neighbors aren't looking, but who cares?). Feel your own continuity with the tree—and, by extension, your loved one's continuity with all created life, including this tree you now embrace in honor and in memory of the one you have lost.

You may be laughing, or crying, or feeling foolish—or some of each. But don't you feel better?

The created world is one and embraces us all, the living and the dead.

Without friends the world is but a wilderness . . . There is no man that imparteth his joys to his friends, but he joyeth the more; and no man that imparteth griefs to his friends, but he grieveth the less.

—FRANCIS BACON

We know this, but sometimes we have to make the effort to prove it to ourselves once again.

Maybe we just don't feel like seeing anyone, not even a friend. Or if we do, maybe we don't want to impose on the friend by going on and on about how terrible this loss is. Or we may not want, just then, to reopen ourselves to this sorrow.

All of these moods are legitimate and we need to honor them. Not all times are appropriate for sharing our grief.

But sometimes with friends, we do take the risk of sharing. Yes, we may cry, and feel the pain of reentering that sorrow, but the fact that we do means there is sorrow there we need to release. And to whom better than to a trusted friend? We will feel more at peace for having done so.

I will trust my friends to hear me in love and understanding.

OCTOBER 31

All shall be well and all shall be well and all manner of thing shall be well.

—JULIAN OF NORWICH

At a time when I thought my world had all but ended, when the realization was hammering at my heart that my daughter's death was not some nightmare from which I would recover but was for all time, a friend came into the room, put her arms around my neck, and said, "Everything's going to be all right."

I thought she was crazy. And yet . . . and yet . . . was it possible that she was right?

I had occasion, some years later, to be the consoler of a young woman whose son had lapsed into a coma from which he would not recover, and my words to her were the same. "Everything's going to be all right." And I felt my friend from that earlier time standing beside me, nodding—*See, that's what I told you.*

Improbable though it seems when grief first assaults us, we do come to learn, though the surface of our life will often be in turmoil, that on a deep and unshakable level there is indeed a confidence that all is well.

Until that happens, we cling to the testimony of others and take hope: if for them, why not for us, too?

All shall be well, and all shall be well, and all manner of thing shall be well.

. . . we talked in a kind of ocean depth of memories where magic fish swam past, as we evoked our parents and Joy's sisters, all dead now but with us for an hour in that exquisite room where time past and time present flowed together.

—MAY SARTON

We often speak of the "communion of saints."

But what we yearn for most particularly, we who have lost loved ones, is to have our own particular "saints" gathered with us. We want to sense that we are present with them and they with us.

People have different experiences of this phenomenon, all the way from hearing voices and seeing ghostly presences to having strong memories of loved ones which call them, almost, to our side. In whatever form this experience occurs, it is a blessing.

But surely among the richest of these experiences are the times when, with nostalgia and often with affectionate laughter, we share with others our memories of someone we love who has gone on before. We leave such experiences warmed and strengthened by our common history, our commemorations of life and of love.

Shared memories can be a source of comfort and joy.

NOVEMBER 2

> Living on memories, clinging to relics and photographs, is an illusion. Like the food offered one in dreams, it will not nourish; no growth or rebirth will come from it.
> —ANNE MORROW LINDBERGH

Many of us know of people who, years after the death of a loved one, will preserve a room "just the way it was," leaving decades-old clothes hanging in a closet, old eyeglasses lying on a table by an open book.

We want a few things that recall a loved one. Better if they are things that have a current use—a mother's favorite teapot in which we now prepare tea, a pen or letter opener that sat on a father's desk and which we now use, a cherished doll that can be passed on to a child who never knew its original owner.

And, of course, pictures. But beware that pictures of the lost loved one aren't the only pictures we display—or that they're present in such numbers that they convey a message that the family's life is back there in a lost era. Shrines have their place, but they are poor backgrounds for life in the present moment.

Lord, grant me the strength to change what can be changed, the grace to accept what cannot be changed, and the wisdom to know the one from the other.

Wilbur's heart brimmed with happiness . . . "Welcome to the barn cellar. You have chosen a hallowed doorway from which to string your webs. I think it is only fair to tell you that I was devoted to your mother . . . I shall always treasure her memory. To you, her daughters, I pledge my friendship, forever and ever."

"I pledge mine," said Joy.

"I do, too," said Aranea.

"And so do I," said Nellie . . .

It was a happy day for Wilbur. And many more happy, tranquil days followed.

—E. B. WHITE

In this beloved children's story, *Charlotte's Web,* we see one of the secrets of healing from grief—the passing on of one's love for the departed to others who come after. In this case it's to Charlotte's daughters that Wilbur's love flows; it could be anyone in need.

How well we know the world brims with people who need attention, care, love! If we have been blessed with a good relationship, now distanced by death, it is an honorable and praiseworthy legacy of that relationship to pass our love on. We never stop loving the one who is gone, and we will help our own healing and enhance the lives of others if, in some way, we open our arms to someone in need.

I know I have love to share. I will be on the lookout.

NOVEMBER 4

Feeling light within, I walk.

—NAVAJO NIGHT CHANT

Each of us carries a light within, though often it seems shrouded in darkness. But it is there—that spark that causes us to respond to love, care, beauty, and need in the world, even when we are sad. Perhaps, indeed, when we are sad we react with even more intensity to the gifts and opportunities life offers.

But can we mobilize ourselves to *walk*, made courageous by that light within? Sometimes, especially when we are grieving, we hang back, fearful. Feeling immobilized, we want someone else to take the initiative.

We have more power than we give ourselves credit for. We will learn the extent of that power only by claiming it and stepping forth. Are we afraid of failure? What have we to fear that can compare with what we have already lost?

So let's take a deep breath and let the sense of that light within burn steady. Then let's move on into our lives, imagining that the one we have lost is helping fan that flame and is cheering us on.

Conscious of my own light and power, I move on into my life.

While grief is fresh, every attempt to divert only irritates.
—JAMES BOSWELL

It is probably well-meaning—this attempt to help a mourner "think of something else," "get your mind off it." As though we could think of something else, when grief is fresh. The well-meaning attempt may also be the comforter's uneasiness about what to say. Never mind that a supportive listening presence is more important than "the right words."

But for the mourner this attempt to divert us can be agonizing. We may feel a kind of panic, as though the person we are speaking with is not connecting, is glancing off at the wings while the main act is being totally ignored. Yet we want to be polite; we know the person is trying to be helpful. So we nod, and smile, and feel an emptiness within, knowing it is costing us valuable energy to maintain this farce.

What to do? Maybe we can steer the conversation around to what is really on both our minds. If not, it's probably better to let the situation run its course. Someone more understanding may come along soon. And at least we'll know what to do when it becomes our turn to be the comforter.

May I bear lightly the words of the well-meaning but inept. They are probably doing their best.

NOVEMBER 6

In this month of thanksgiving, we can be thankful for the trials of the past, the blessings of the present, and be heartily ready at the same time to embrace with joy any troubles the future may bring.

—DOROTHY DAY

Well, maybe. Surely we are grateful for the blessings of the present. And perhaps we have made our peace with the trials of the past—or at least we're working on it.

But "embrace with joy" the troubles of the future?

One of the things our knowledge of sorrow and pain teaches us is that we can survive. Not only survive, but in the experience we are made stronger—so that the next time sorrow and pain come our way, maybe we can greet them with more courage, more confidence—even a kind of distilled joy that as sharers in the human community, we can make it through.

When we are in the grip of fresh grief, our response is probably, Who cares? This kind of wisdom is bought at too high a price. We don't want it. We can't imagine ever being thankful—for *this*?

Not for this—no. But perhaps we can look to the time when the survival strengths we gain will stand us in good stead.

I am grateful for the blessings of the present. As to the future—I'll wait and see.

Open your eyes and see those things which are around us at this hour.

—RICHARD JEFFRIES

One of our temptations when our lives are shaken by grief is to live—nostalgically or regretfully—in the past.

Another is to live—in mournful projection—in the future.

It is sometimes said of "feeling types" (as opposed to "thinking types") that they have to be dragged "kicking and screaming" into the present moment.

When we are grieving the loss of a loved one, we are most apt to be in a "feeling type" mode. We may need to take ourselves in hand—putting blinders on our inner eye so we look only at what is present to us now. There is no fear that we will lose our memory of the past or our sense of the future. Each will be there, ready for our regret, our yearning, our hovering attention.

But for now, for this hour—or even for this fifteen minutes—let's open our eyes, wherever we are, turn *very* slowly in a full circle, and see what there is to see!

For this moment, the place where I am is my world.

November 8

If at times we are somewhat stunned by the tempest,
never fear; let us take breath, and go on afresh.
—Francis de Sales

Grieving is such a roller-coaster ride. One day we think
the worst is over, that we're really beginning to pick up
our lives again. The next day—or the next hour!—it's as
though it was all fresh, and we have made no progress at
all.

We need to remember that recovery from grief is not a
smooth uphill path. There will be many setbacks, many
side paths onto which we are led, before we can continue
our journey out of the valley of sadness.

Better not waste our energy castigating ourselves that
we're not "doing better." We're doing as well as we can,
and these "tempests" and setbacks are all part of the process. So let us expect them, accept them when they come,
then take a deep breath and move on.

*I will not be discouraged by the mood swings of grieving, but
realize they are part of the road to health.*

Have courage for the great sorrows of life and patience for the small ones; and when you have laboriously accomplished your daily task, go to sleep in peace. God is awake.

—VICTOR HUGO

We feel the weight of grief so heavily. There are tasks to perform. Not to mention all the emotional weighing and reweighing we do. We find it hard to relax, to achieve any tranquility, to sleep—though we know nothing is gained by all this mental agitation.

There is a story about a man called Charles Carter who was involved in many good works. One day he felt himself becoming ill. In great distress he thought, "I can't be sick now. I have too much to do, too many people depending on me." But he did go to sleep, and in his sleep he had a dream in which he saw the Lord God Almighty pacing the floor of Heaven, wringing His hands and saying, "What shall I do? What shall I do? Charles Carter is going to be sick."

The world is not in our hands, and when we find ourselves squeezed in a vise of our own anguish, let's try to release all that, give it into the hands of One who is the source of all power and love, who neither slumbers nor sleeps.

I will give over this turmoil in my mind, and be at peace.

November 10

For when is death not within ourselves? . . . Living and dead are the same, and so are awake and asleep, young and old.

—Heraclitus

When we lose a loved one, we feel such a fracturing of our lives, a sense of being separated—as though our experience and the loved one's are now forever different.

Perhaps it is a strange comfort to remember that we are all part of the same human adventure, that our loved one has gone on ahead, on a path that we shall follow.

But this may be a source of anxiety and fear, too. We are reminded of our own mortality. How will death be for us? We hear stories that affirm a life after death beautiful beyond imagining, and we turn to these stories as a thirsty person craves water.

On the other hand . . . while life has its hard moments, it is also wonderful. We have others we love; we are in no hurry.

So all our apprehensions as well as our hopes for life beyond death are brought into focus by the death of a loved one. To be close to another's journey enlarges our own view of life and death, and hopefully, death becomes a door, not a wall.

As I think of my loved one, I know that the same stream of creation embraces us all.

. . . and it was gray, and grayer the deeper he went. What if it was deeper than he had figured? But soon the light changed, the muck brightened, and he was headed out, towards clear sky and sun again. He said that was the best sight in the world: the world.

—JOSEPHINE HUMPHRIES

Deeper and deeper we burrow into our grief. Desolations pile on one another. We wonder if we shall ever see anything on the horizon but this gloom and sadness.

Then one day, in some moment of quiet reflection, we find ourselves Thinking of Something Else! Is it possible?

We will move back and forth many times—back into the dark woods and forward again into light. After a while we will realize it is all one world, that feelings of joy and sadness enrich each other—as a person who has been mortally ill has a new appreciation for the beauty of starlight, the taste of orange juice, the caress of love.

Is it all right? Is it being disloyal to our lost loved one—to savor our life afresh? Are we in danger of forgetting? Not to worry. We would as soon forget to breathe.

I will be open to the possibility of joy in my life, and I will not be afraid.

November 12

Give unto them beauty for ashes, the oil of joy for mourning, the garment of praise for the spirit of heaviness.

—Isaiah 61:3

The Prophet is anticipating the good news of God's deliverance. Of what does deliverance consist for us?

Not that the situation will change and our loved one be restored to us. We know better than to hope for that.

But maybe to be delivered from some of this pain, so that our existence is no longer shadowed by our loss, and the beauty of the world is no longer just a reminder that the one we shared it with is gone. From that—yes—we can hope to be delivered.

We have but to look around us and see the many others who have suffered losses. They are legion. They walk the streets with us, get on and off the bus, shop with us in the stores. They have survived. And some of them have been made stronger and are now pillars of support for others.

When we shall have been delivered from our deepest grief—by the help of friends, by faith, by time, by work to which we can return with a heightened sensibility—then we, too, shall experience "beauty for ashes, the oil of joy for mourning, the garment of praise for the spirit of heaviness," and be a blessing to those who need us.

I know that I shall walk out into the sunshine again.

It is important, when dealing with all aspects of grief, to keep the process moving. The temptation is to freeze, to stay perpetually recoiled against so terrible a blow.
—MARTHA WHITMORE HICKMAN

It is almost a physical sensation, especially if death has come suddenly and unexpectedly—almost a sense of having the wind knocked out of you. And even if death has been a long time in coming, there is an impulse to dig in one's feet at the moment of death. It is our last experience of our loved one and we want to hold on, keep the immediacy of that memory from growing dim.

That's all right for a while. But the danger is that we will get stuck there. All of us have known or heard of people who keep a room just as it was while the loved one was alive—even to the point of slippers resting beside a favorite chair and clothes hanging in the closet. This does not honor the truth—either of our own lives or that of our loved one. Wherever he or she is, it is certainly not "back there." Bit by bit, we need to loosen our hold on a past we cannot keep and get on with the life we have.

As I move on into my new life, can I think of my loved one as doing the same?

NOVEMBER 14

Even in the dark you have the power to whistle.
—FREDERICK BUECHNER

It seems a simple thing—to muster the will and energy to whistle.

But one of the major components of grief is that it's hard to lift one's voice—or whistle—in song. It's also hard to do anything that requires us to take the initiative. We tend to be reactive, not to initiate. To claim our power at all is a victory, and to do something associated with a carefree state of mind—like whistling—is a major victory. It may signify a great change in the range of moods we're willing to experience. We are ready to give up the image of ourselves as the dolorous and wounded and, for this moment anyway, rejoin the active stream of human life.

So if we're able to whistle—or do anything that seems to distance us from our consuming burden of grief—it's not only a song, it's a milestone. We're on the move, laying down our encompassing cloak of I Am the Wounded One, and moving out. It's a triumph. It's something to whistle about!

Bit by bit, I am walking out of the dark.

Guests of my life,
You came in the early dawn, and you in the night.
Your name was uttered by the Spring flowers and yours by the showers of rain.
You brought the harp into my house and you brought the lamp.
After you had taken your leave I found God's footprints on my floor.

—RABINDRANATH TAGORE

It is so easy to think we have some ultimate claim on those we love, rather than that we have been privileged to share one another's lives for a time—they with us, and we with them.

We know that we pass on our genes to our descendants, as our parents have passed theirs on to us. We orally pass on our memories and leave behind times we've shared with those we love.

But always there is some essence which is at its heart a mystery. And where it came from and where it goes, we don't know. But perhaps there is a trace of the divine in each of us, which comes from its home in God, and returns to that home.

Before the mystery of life I am silent, and glad.

NOVEMBER 16

. . . And I knew . . .
That when the sea comes calling you stop being good
neighbors,
Well acquainted, friendly from a distance neighbors,
And you give your house for a coral castle,
And you learn to breathe under water.

—CAROL BIALOCK

We've known that death is a part of life. We've been present to grieving friends—maybe passed through other grief experiences ourselves. But each experience of grief is new, always asks its own questions, demands its own answers. Even when the loss of a loved one comes after a long illness, so that we are "prepared," and surely when death comes suddenly, without warning, we must step over into a new country. The colors are different, the air has a different feel, and the sounds have a different echo from what they had before.

There is, now, nothing academic, philosophically removed and comfortable about it. "Of course I know everyone has to die" becomes a sudden intake of breath, a casting about for "What do I do now? What do I do next?" And we learn the colors and sounds of this new world, and after a while it becomes our world.

Somewhere deep in my being is the seed of peace.

Everything in life that we really accept undergoes a change. So suffering must become love. That is the mystery.

—KATHERINE MANSFIELD

It doesn't happen right away. We are too preoccupied with our own deprivation and sadness. And we need time to mull over our lives, to go over and over what we have lost, what we are going to do, what the future may hold.

And it probably doesn't happen—that suffering becomes love—because we will it so.

But all the time we are struggling with our grief and its meaning, the seeds of a new compassion are germinating in our psyches. Because we have suffered, we are tender-hearted toward others. Because our own defenses have been peeled away, we have a new perspective on what it means to be vulnerable, and we recognize the vulnerability of others. Because we recognize how closely we are all connected to one another, in a way we become porous, transparent—people whom the light shines through.

And the light, which is love illuminated, reaches those around us and perhaps they, too, become able to take the risk of loving. Together we realize that "no man [or woman] is an island." We know that, while we are still sad, we are not alone, and that love, often forged out of sadness, is life's greatest gift to us all.

Love is a mystery in which I dwell, grateful and unafraid.

November 18

I don't really remember the day I first felt that all was not irremediably lost. Was it a child's smile that awoke me, or a sign of sadness exposed in a place I didn't want it seen? Or a sense of responsibility? Or had I finally given up on despair? Perhaps I was simply caught up again in the game of life.

—ANNE PHILIPE

It comes as a surprise to us. Almost, we never thought it would happen. But one day we realize we are taking pleasure in the world once more. It is doubly a gift—this rediscovery of the joy of life—because we thought it was gone from us forever.

And there it is—like early spring flowers, pushing their way through March's lingering snow. They are an unexpected gift and their beauty calls our attention to new life all around us.

My step quickens, my heart leaps in gratitude, for the surprising return of the beauty in the world.

We are, perhaps uniquely among the world's creatures, the worrying animal. We worry away our lives, fearing the future, discontent with the present, unable to take in the idea of dying, unable to sit still.

—LEWIS THOMAS

Easier said than done, to get rid of all that.

But we do recognize its wisdom—the futility of worrying, the danger of being so agitated toward life that we can't savor the wonders of the moment, can't even sit still!

Fred Buechner has written about "the family worrier"— the one who takes on the worries about money and health and schedules and the durability of the family car, thereby freeing the others for more spontaneous and joyous pursuits.

Perhaps, for a breather—anytime, but maybe particularly when we feel burdened with heavy grief—we can make a conscious decision to "give it over," as the early believers used to say—give to God (or the air, or some strong, stalwart tree) the whole swirling current of our grief and our agonizing about the meaning of life and death, and just drink in the moment!

Worry has been described as the ultimate self-indulgence. I don't need it!

NOVEMBER 20

Take time to plan your future . . . If it is financially possible for you, stay in your own home, with the familiar things around you.

Later, if you go away, if you travel, even if you decide to make your home elsewhere, the spirit of tenderness, of love, will not desert you. You will find that it has become part of you, rising from within yourself; and because of it you are no longer fearful of loneliness, of the dark, because death, the last enemy, has been overcome.

—DAPHNE DU MAURIER

The painter Andrew Wyeth, when asked why he didn't travel around more, is reputed to have said, "The familiar frees me."

Perhaps the familiar also frees us to grieve, even as it wraps around us with memory and its own comfort.

Or it may keep us in bondage. After her husband's death, a friend removed from her house almost immediately the old brown chair he most often sat in. It was one way of acknowledging that he was gone, that her life had entered a new chapter. For someone else, it might have been a comfort to sit in that chair. We each have to find our own way.

I will be careful, knowing the familiar can free me or imprison me.

> True prayer brings us to the edge of a great mystery
> where we become inarticulate, where our knowledge
> fails.
>
> —PARKER PALMER

We would like so much to *know*. Is my loved one in some state of gloriously enhanced being? What is it like? Is he or she aware of me? Shall we know each other again?

If I pray, will I know? But the sustaining power of prayer is not to be found in unanswerable questions.

A few years ago my husband and I went to Alaska. One of the highlights of the tour was a bus ride to Denali (Mount McKinley). We'd heard about its towering majesty all our lives. We were told it was unlikely we'd be able to see it—the sky was apt to be clouded, visibility low.

After several hours the bus turned around the base of a hill. We saw a line of spectators, shoulder to shoulder, gazing across the Alaskan terrain. There was the mountain, miles away—gigantic, white—looming into the sky.

We joined the other spectators—probably a hundred people. There was little conversation. We all gazed at the mountain. And nothing—no words, no pictures in a travel brochure, no statistics—could have prepared us. We were silent.

In the mystery of prayer—I just have to be there.

NOVEMBER 22

You may my glories and my state depose,
But not my griefs. Still I am king of those.
— WILLIAM SHAKESPEARE

Grief is a private matter, as well as a public one, affecting as it does all our relationships with friends, family, and our world.

But it is in our solitude that we are most affected by our loss. It is there, in our interplay with memory and our decisions about our energy and time, that we hold in our hands some control over the course of our grief.

It is a responsibility that sometimes we would as soon not have. It is easy to fall into ruts—even ruts of grieving. We get used to living in this mood, and it may be more comfortable to stay with it than to make the effort to move away from grief as the center of our lives. We may even feel possessive of our grief—as though any attempt, by us or by well-meaning friends, might reduce the importance of our loss, or even of our loved one.

We are the best judges of when to stay in our grief and when to move on to something else. The important thing is to inwardly accept responsibility for the choices we make. And to recognize the difference between grieving over the loss of a loved one and continuing to cherish that person.

Sometimes the best choice is to be in my grief, sometimes not.

I do not know whether human personality survives physical death. I am content to wait and see what comes after death, open to any possibility. If it should turn out to be eternal sleep, that too is a gift after a full life.

—ELIZABETH WATSON

This seems small comfort when we are caught up in fresh grief at the loss of a loved one. A part of our life has been severed, and we long desperately for that relationship.

There is no way to know in what terms that may be possible after death. But as time passes, we see that, even in the physical absence of the loved one, the relationship does resume, as we sense the person's influence and presence with us in subtle and pervasive ways.

As for the possibility that death is eternal sleep . . . think of the tiredest you have ever been and how inviting sleep was. Is that so bad? Especially when you know the essence of who you were will be with your loved ones for the rest of their lives.

Having no alternative . . . I will trust life with what I cannot know.

NOVEMBER 24

> . . . the astonishing or unfortunate thing is that these dep-
> rivations bring us the cure at the same time that they give
> rise to pain. Once we have accepted the fact of loss, we
> understand that the loved one obstructed a whole corner
> of the possible, pure now as a sky washed by rain . . .
> Free, we seek anew, enriched by pain. And the perpetual
> impulse forward always falls back again to gather new
> strength. The fall is brutal, but we set out again.
> —ALBERT CAMUS

It is a trade we would never willingly have made, and for
a while the "corner of the possible" is nothing but grieving. We have no impulse toward new things.

But when some time has passed and we are able to
stand back a bit from our grief and look at our lives, we
do find some empty space where our involvement with
our loved one used to be.

What to do with that time and energy? Maybe it will be
subsumed into other things we're already doing. Or
maybe it is time to consider something new. Perhaps in
the transfer of the energy we used to give to our relationship we can see a living memorial to our loved one. Let's
make it something worthwhile!

*My life is entering a new chapter. What new thing shall I put
into it?*

Something within me is waking from long sleep, and I want to live and move again. Some zest is returning to me, some immense gratefulness for those who love me, some strong wish to love them also. I am full of thanks for life. I have not told myself to be thankful. I just am so.
—ALAN PATON

It is like returning to health when one has been desperately sick. Each day seems a gift—the sun brighter, the air clearer, the taste of food a wonder on the tongue.

The word "rebirth" is not too strong a word for this return to happiness, to deep contentment with life. But it is in some ways a different world into which we are reborn. There are things we recognize from the world we knew—the same furniture, the same town, most of the same people—but everything has a new coloration. The foundation has tilted, threatened to slide us into the abyss, then righted itself. We are the stronger now for having survived the storm.

Because it seems a new world, time almost slows down, as it did when we were children. And our gratitude for the wonders of this world is almost as profound and simple as a child's—gratitude for a world washed with our tears, as fresh now as a landscape after rain.

To come through great sorrow is to be reborn into a new world.

NOVEMBER 26

So he passed over, and all the trumpets sounded for him
on the other side.

—JOHN BUNYAN

If we believe in a life after death, which images play
around that belief? Victorian images hardly seem plausible—or appealing. "Heavenly choirs" aroused antipathy
in Mark Twain, who wondered why we pictured Heaven
as including all those things we could hardly abide while
alive. No sex. Heavenly choirs. Please!

John Bunyan's image in *Pilgrim's Progress* seems old-fashioned in some ways.

But what has fashion to do with it? It is all conjecture—
attempts to express the unknowable.

Modern images have to do with light—a tunnel, perhaps, and then light! Always warmth. Always inconceivably wonderful love. For many, the faces of loved ones. A
figure of God, or some other religious embodiment.

Who knows? But the sound of trumpets welcoming a
triumphant spiritual warrior home is not bad. What music
were they playing? We'll have to wait and see.

*In my fantasy I am reaching for the welcoming arms of my loved
one.*

In search of my mother's garden, I found my own.
—ALICE WALKER

At a time of loss, our heritage—that succession of genes and circumstance that brought us into being—assumes even greater importance in our minds. Or maybe it's that everything that's important becomes more important with the intensity of feeling that loss brings on.

We may cherish anew our forebears, savoring who they were and what they have passed on to us, not only physical characteristics like eye color and body shape, but things like a gift for math, a love of gardening, or even favorite foods. Growing up, I felt an immeasurably strengthened bond with my grandmother when my mother said, "You're like my mother. Pears were her favorite fruit, too." The fact that I bore her name added to that bond. These things made me feel like her close companion, though she died when I was two. So we strengthen our ties of love and take comfort from the networks of history of which we and our loved ones are a part.

I rejoice in the rich fabric of family and friends which holds me safe, and grateful, at a time like this.

NOVEMBER 28

The light died in the low clouds. Falling snow drank in the dusk. Shrouded in silence, the branches wrapped me in their peace. When the boundaries were erased, once again the wonder: that *I* exist.

—DAG HAMMARSKJÖLD

Maybe in the wake of great sorrow, sensitized as we are to the shadings and symbolisms of experience, to the mysteries at the edges of life, we are more able than at other times to feel a kind of unifying pulse with all that is.

I remember, in the aftermath of a great sorrow, standing on a mountaintop veranda on a clear summer night and feeling as though there was an almost palpable connection between me and the stars above the opposite mountain peak that shone in the night sky.

This tenderness toward creation is a gift dearly bought, and perhaps it's a kind of expanded consciousness evoked by our reaching out into the universe for what we have lost: *Where are you? Do you read me? Do you see me standing here, thinking of you? I love you. I know you know that.*

On and on it can go, this fantasy conversation with the dead. And yet, in the unity of life, who knows who is speaking and who is listening?

I will be still in my soul, and think of my love.

God is coming to us. But in order for that truly to happen, we must go as well to God. The highway runs in two directions. The invitation is for the divine and human to meet halfway.

—WENDY WRIGHT

As with any relationship, it takes some interest, some willingness, on both sides. Not that—whatever our idea of God—we could imagine a God who hangs back, shy or even petulant, waiting to be noticed.

But if we are turned the other way so we cannot see, if our ears are stopped so we cannot hear, it is unlikely we can be aware of a God who waits eagerly to comfort and reassure us.

What does that say to us who grieve and are hungry for any support, any inkling of a God who loves us and cares for us in the midst of our sorrow?

Perhaps that we have to at least entertain the possibility that God is out there, waiting.

And as we would wait for the sound of expected guests to drive up to our door and then rush out to meet them and welcome them in, let us, if some mood of expectancy and faith comes over us, abandon ourselves to that possibility—and see how the conversation goes!

Any relationship requires the participation of both sides.

November 30

Into Paradise may the angels in whom I do not believe
lead thee; at thy coming may the martyrs long decom-
posed take thee up, in eternal rest, and may the chorus
of angels lead thee to that which does not exist, the holy
city, and perpetual light.

—William Gibson

There is a way in which reason fights against the possibility of life beyond death. We see the body suddenly devoid of life, of spirit. Where has it gone? We do not want
to be duped, even for our own comfort. How can a spirit
live without its lifetime clothing?

And yet . . . we want so badly to believe there is more,
and that we shall know one another again. The religions
of humankind have described a frame for us on which we
can hang belief. We have stories, hunches, hopes. We have
visitations and dreams, and we know of lives made over
by the force of what cannot be seen or measured.

So to be on the safe side, we express our uncertainty,
our skepticism, and then from somewhere comes the in-
tuitive flash of faith, and the stories, and we are lifted up
on wings . . . and we fly!

Faith is a gift. I can open my hands to receive it.

Be reverent before the dawning day. Do not think of what
will be in a year, or in ten years. Think of today.
—ROMAIN ROLLAND

It is hard, at any time of life, not to be unduly concerned
with what lies ahead. But when we have lost a loved one,
it is doubly hard. All the plans and hope we had for a
future in which that person continued to figure have to be
reshaped. Even if the loved person has died in old age,
the future still has to be recast. If it's a parent who has
died, the remove of that buffer between us and death has
its own sobering meaning: How will it be for me, being
the older generation? How will it be in ten years—or
twenty—when I am "the old person"? Will others be there
for me? If one's child has died, the reversal of sequence in
the human drama evokes all kinds of anticipated pain
about a future that should have been different.

And in the meantime, while we are worrying and fret-
ting and feeling sorry for ourselves, life slips away.

It is a hard discipline to adopt—and we can't do it all
the time—but let's try to greet each day as its own gift—
or its own trial if it's that kind of a day. But let's not bury
the sunshine and beauty of this day under the shadow of
a regretted future—about whose nature we can only spec-
ulate.

*I will look around me now, this minute, and see what my life
holds.*

DECEMBER 2

There is a gravitational pull, an endless current which we do not recognize which draws us beyond all things and people, but at the same time more deeply and freely into them.

—EDWARD J. FARRELL

One of the ambiguous gifts of our suffering (and they are ambiguous: they are gifts, and we would never have chosen them) is that it enlarges our perspective. Petty complaints we had seem unimportant. People with whom we thought we had nothing in common become special friends. Vocational prowess drops down on the list of our life's priorities; relationships are what matter.

At the same time that we feel more profoundly and gratefully connected to friends and family, we have a sense that all of us dwell in mystery, that we are connected to earth and sky, to the rhythms of the universe, to the whole range of living things in ways we do not understand.

Maybe I can relinquish my "white knuckle" grip on life, and trust that all will be well.

I was beginning to do better, I thought I was doing better, but a few days ago the holidays just hit me.
—WIDOW, CONTEMPLATING HER FIRST CHRISTMAS ALONE

Memories are always there to hook us, to make the grief fresh again—birthdays, anniversaries, summer vacation—any occasion of "the first time around" without our loved one. But the Christmas holidays, the Hanukkah observances, when the whole world seems poised for celebration, are among the most difficult times of year for survivors of loss. Each of us has a time-honored list of things "we always do"—go to services, hang the stockings, light the candles, share traditional foods. They are part of our identity and our joy in being alive in the world together—and now one of the key people with whom we shared that joy is gone. Is it any wonder we cringe from the thought of the holidays?

We will get through it, and probably better if we can talk about it with others who are feeling the same loss. Reaching out to others (the poor, the lonely, the homeless) for whom this is also a difficult season will help, and will express the deeper meaning of the season.

◆◆

I know this will be a hard season for me. I will take one day at a time. I will acknowledge when grief hovers close. And I will try to be open to times when joy may surprise me, too.

December 4

There are seasons of prayer which, though spent amid distractions and tediousness, are yet, owing to a good intention, fruitful to the heart, strengthening it against all temptation.
—FRANCOIS DE SALIGNAC DE LA MOTHE FÉNELON

The temptation for mourners is to despair. There are other temptations—to deny, to idealize, to refuse help—just to name a few. But despair is certainly readily available, and especially so at this season when everyone is gearing up for holiday celebrations and family get-togethers. And if we are trying to keep our hearts and minds "on track" for healing, there are extra difficulties at this time—distractions galore, and too much to do. We get overtired, and our sadness permeates it all, making the burden heavier.

Now is a good time to heed the words of the seventeenth-century author and churchman, Fénelon. We can acknowledge the difficulties of the season, do what we can to cultivate some inner peace, and trust that we won't lose our way before the sometime-glad, sometime-sad weeks pass and things quiet down.

In the flurry of the coming weeks I will try to spend a few minutes each day in prayerful silence—my own particular stay against the emotional and physical tumult of these days.

What we call mourning for our dead is perhaps not so much grief at not being able to call them back as it is grief at not being able to want to do so.

—THOMAS MANN

These are hard words when we are struggling with all the feelings that go with the loss of a loved one. The suggestion that there are pluses to his or her being gone may be offensive in the extreme. But what Mann is talking about is the ambivalence that attends any relationship, even the most cherished and loving.

Does this mean we didn't love the person? No! Or that, if he or she could be well and able, in the balance we wouldn't want him or her back? In most cases, no. (The person might not want to come back, either!) It means that the equations of human relationships are wonderfully complex—as we know when we take an honest look in the mirror.

To love someone profoundly is to know that person in his or her weakness and strength.

DECEMBER 6

Piece by piece, I reenter the world. A new phase. A new body, a new voice. Birds console me by flying, trees by growing, dogs by the warm patch they leave on the sofa. Unknown people merely by performing their motions. It's like a slow recovery from a sickness, this recovery of one's self.

—TOBY TALBOT

Back when our grief was fresh, we thought this would never happen—that we would take pleasure in the small, ordinary events of life. Back then, we thought our perception of the world would always be dominated by this piercing, overriding loss. So we're twice blessed when, a bit at a time, we begin to savor once more the lovely ongoing processes by which life is quietly fostered, day by day. We're twice blessed because the sharp teeth of our loss no longer bite into our consciousness all the time, and because we're aware of the wonderful life-sustaining things going on around us—like red cardinals against a winter snow or the warmth of fire when we have come in from the cold. We used to take these for granted. Then nothing was to be taken for granted anymore. And now perhaps we—even we—can relax into the everyday and begin to trust life again.

I will open my eyes and stretch out my arms to the beauty and wonder of the world.

What's gone and what's past help
Should be past grief.

—WILLIAM SHAKESPEARE

Ah, but it isn't! That's part of what the grief is all about—
that there's no changing what's happened, no help available for restoring what's gone.

Shakespeare's character Paulina, from *The Winter's Tale*, admonishes with a message no more palatable to her listener than a modern counterpart would be to us: "Cheer up. It's over. You can't do anything to change it. Just accept it and go ahead with your life."

It's bad enough if we hear this kind of advice from well-meaning friends. It's worse yet if we regale ourselves with such exhortations and feel guilty if we can't act on them.

Of course we don't want to mope around, grieving forever. But the surest way to avoid that is not to put caps on the wells of our grief and try to walk away, but to deal with grief honestly, experiencing its pain and anger for as long as we need to. Then and only then will we be able to incorporate the meaning of our loss into our lives, and move ahead.

Assimilating this loss into my life is a long process, and I will give it its due.

DECEMBER 8

When I asked the orthopedic surgeon who treated me whether people often fracture bones after bereavement, he said, without even looking up from my injured foot, "Naturally, people lose their sense of balance."

—LILY PINCUS

Sometimes it's not as specific as that—the body reacting with its own wounds to a wound of mind and spirit. But it is well known that after a serious loss, our bodies are more prone to injury and disease. So it behooves us to take particularly good care of ourselves—to be more careful about diet, about driving when we're tired, and to try to get some extra rest.

Do we have more accidents because we're depressed and don't care as much about keeping ourselves healthy—even keeping ourselves alive? Are we careless because we're preoccupied with grief? Is there something in the chemistry of grief that affects our immune system and makes it harder for our bodies to fight infection? The relationship between mind and body is being examined as never before, and there's much that we don't know.

But we do know we are at extra risk, and in deference to ourselves and to those we love, we would do well to take the best care of ourselves that we can.

I have much to live for, and I'll live for it better if I'm healthy!

When everything is dark, when we are surrounded by despairing voices, when we do not see any exits, then we can find salvation in a remembered love, a love which is not simply a recollection of a bygone past but a living force which sustains us in the present. Through memory, love transcends the limits of time and offers hope at any moment of our lives.

—HENRI NOUWEN

I remember, as an adolescent, watching a Catholic friend "say" her rosary beads—touching each in turn while saying the prescribed prayer. I was intrigued and puzzled—this expression of faith was far from my free church Protestant heritage in which we did nothing by rote except murmur the Lord's Prayer each Sunday.

But the image of precious beads on a string has stayed with me, and I sometimes think of treasured memories in this way. The time my husband and I had just started dating and I told him I was going to a distant city and he thought I meant for good; the look on his face when he said, "I'm sorry to hear that," is a memory I have treasured for more than forty years. Or the time my daughter expressing her pride in a poem I had written, asked, "Can I take it to school and show it to my teacher?"

The love emanating from my memories is eternal.

DECEMBER 10

Even as I stood there, the tears streaming down my face, I felt a kind of joy for him, a strange gaiety almost, that he would so soon be released, and I had a sense that he stood now on the threshold of some great adventure . . . So it was in a strange way not only a time of terrible sorrow, but a moment of light, as I stood there telling him goodbye.

—MARTHA WHITMORE HICKMAN

It was my father who lay on the bed, dying. I had expected the sorrow. Though I have faith in a life beyond death, I had not expected the strange rush of happiness, the expectation of adventure and joy. Not right then. So it was all the more a gift, though a fleeting one.

None of us knows what lies on the other side of death, but we have had clues—in stories handed down, in experiences of our own, in books detailing near-death experiences—that offer great hope and promise that beyond death are light and welcome and unimaginable peace and joy. What comfort these clues can be to us on the dark days. We pore over them as over rosary beads—Yes, we think. Hope is justified. Everything will turn out right in the end.

In my times of darkness, lead me to the light.

Weeping may linger for the night, but joy comes with the morning.

—PSALM 30

How many times have we lain awake at night, our thoughts weighted with stress, our brains whirring over this or that problem, and all of it compounded by our frustration at not being able to do what we should be doing—which is to sleep! And then in the morning, though we may be tired, things usually do look better.

To be in profound grief is a much more basic affliction than a little nocturnal restlessness, but it does seem as though grief sits more heavily on our hearts when all is still and dark. A good time to cry. Sometimes an unavoidable time to cry.

Then the morning comes. And even though the sadness persists into daylight, perhaps it moderates a bit with the sight of sunshine, the smell of coffee, some familiar routines to attend to.

Not to mention the symbolic overtones of night and morning—that, grim though our sadness is, surely there are brighter days ahead!

◆◆

I will welcome the sunshine into my life—for warmth, for illumination, and as a bearer of hope.

December 12

> Dead and gone though they may be, as we come to understand them in new ways, it is as though they come to understand us—and through them we come to understand ourselves—in new ways, too.
>
> —Frederick Buechner

This delicate dance with the souls of the dead is something we don't begin to understand right away. We think the immediate relationship is ended, though we know we will continue to remember, and to grieve.

But as we dwell in memory on our experiences with the one who is physically gone, his or her psychic presence, rather than being confined to the body we knew and loved, seems somehow to expand and surround us with its gentle understanding, its compassion and love.

So we enter upon different kinds of conversations, often exchanges without words. We seem to arrive at a mutual understanding and appreciation for the goodness and the difficulty we were in each other's life. We're able to smile benevolently at all that flurry and to relish, instead, this deep love and peace.

Dear departed love, continue to be with me, as I will with you.

I feel a strong immortal hope,
which bears my mournful spirit up
beneath its mountain load;
redeemed from death, and grief, and pain,
I soon shall find my friend again
within the arms of God.

—CHARLES WESLEY

Our images come from our experiences. The image of being cradled in the arms of God is an old and much-used analogy of a love as primal, as necessary, as that of a parent cradling an infant child. What greater security could we imagine?

If we have been parents ourselves, we know how that feels, and that a parent's need to cradle a helpless newborn child is as strong as the infant's need to be held. If we have not been parents, we have certainly witnessed—in friends and family—this kind of tenderness, of absolute mutual attention. What better could we hope for than that our loved one who has gone on into death is welcomed by a love as nurturing, as all-embracing, as that—a love to which we, too, shall be heirs when it is our time to go?

I commend my dear one to the arms of the all-embracing love.

DECEMBER 14

I stand under the golden canopy of thine evening sky and I lift my eager eyes to thy face.

I have come to the brink of eternity from which nothing can vanish—no hope, no happiness, no vision of a face seen through tears.

Oh, dip my emptied life into that ocean, plunge it into the deepest fullness. Let me for once feel that lost sweet touch in the allness of the universe.

—RABINDRANATH TAGORE

This vision of an eternity in which nothing is lost can be a great comfort to us. For though our loved one may be separated from us for a time, we feel that we are all part of the encompassing Oneness of creation, and that when we, too, pass over the brink of eternity, we will experience that ultimate fullness in which our loved one abides—and so shall we.

This hope, this picture of recovered love in the midst of universal light and love, is so much a part of the world view of so many individuals and so many communities—surely there must be something to it!

In the unity of creation I can hope to find my love again.

Bless Thou to be mine eye.
May mine eye bless all it sees;
I will bless my neighbour,
May my neighbour bless me.

—CELTIC PRAYER

How we are all bound together—all in need of one another's blessing!

It might be helpful, as we wend our way through this day, if we made a conscious effort to offer a silent blessing on behalf of all the people we meet. It will surely do them no harm, and it will help us approach them with a maximum of understanding and good will.

And who knows—they may pick up from us the energy of our thoughts toward them and respond to us with unusual sensitivity and grace. (We can't count on it, and if it doesn't happen, it won't invalidate our impulse on their behalf. At the least, the goodwill in the world will have gone up by a few tiny increments!)

I will bless my neighbor. May my neighbor bless me.

DECEMBER 16

"You will embark," he said, "on a fair sea, and at times there will be fair weather, but not always. You will meet storms and overcome them. You will take it in turns to steer your boat through fair weather and foul. Never lose courage. Safe harbour awaits you both in the end."
—DAPHNE DU MAURIER

The relationship described here is a long and happy marriage, but it could be any long-term relationship between those who love each other. And what more could we hope for, looking back over the vagaries, the "fair weather and foul," through which any long and intense relationship goes, than this recognition that we have met storms and not been overcome, and that safe harbor awaits us both at the end?

Seldom do two people who love each other reach harbor at the same time. One gets there first. In our case, in this relationship, we will arrive second. And it is not too much to hope that this one we loved—and other loved ones who have gone before us—will be present at the harbor, waiting to welcome us home.

With confidence in the stars that guide me and the waves that carry me, I move toward that harbor where my loved ones wait.

The supreme value is not the future but the present.
—OCTAVIO PAZ

The present is bad enough when we are hit with fresh grief. But we compound our sorrow by spinning our minds out over all the years and occasions of the future when we will so sorely miss the presence of our loved one.

A certain amount of this is not only inevitable, but helpful—a kind of rehearsal for what lies ahead, and a way of getting used to our loss by thinking of all its ramifications.

But after a while we need to remind ourselves that life is lived one day at a time, and that this day, this present moment, is all we have, all we can be sure of. Sir William Osler speaks of living our lives in "day-tight compartments"—as a ship's captain, with the touch of a button, shuts off parts of that ship into watertight compartments.

It is we who control the buttons of our own preoccupations and concerns, and we will do much better if we focus most of our attention on the moments and hours of the day that is before us.

I will try to contend graciously and productively with this day.

DECEMBER 18

> Therefore it is not God's will that when we feel pain we should pursue it in sorrow and mourning over it, but that suddenly we should pass it over, and preserve ourselves in the endless delight which is God.
>
> —JULIAN OF NORWICH

Easier said than done, right?

Sometimes we may feel, on some level, that if we relinquish our grieving, the work of grieving will be neglected, our loved one honored less than he or she deserves, our own grief somehow not given enough weight.

But maybe, at least for a time, we can step back from our grief and in a way "trust the universe" to take care of it. If creation is one, then no grief—as no joy—is lost. We need to grieve, but our loved one does not need that from us. Nor does God need for us, in our small corner of the universe, to restore the balance of the world by matching our grief to the degree of our loss.

Think of the phrase in traditional folk religion: "Give it over"—hand it to God. By so doing, lighten your burden, confident that God knows better than we what to do with all that—probably has already done it.

If we can put our trust in God, then, after our grieving, we can return to life with confidence and joy.

What is there to do when people die—people so dear
and rare—but bring them back by remembering?
—MAY SARTON

One of the truly helpful customs of recent years is that of
providing an occasion—in the context of a memorial service or in some other specified setting—where mourners
are encouraged to share memories of the one who has
died. There will be tears. There may be laughter. There
will certainly be a sense of richness as the person is remembered, his or her nature and history celebrated.

This process will go on and on—at gatherings of family
and friends, at random times when a story comes to mind
and is shared. This is invariably a lift. Even when the stories are not particularly complimentary, they bring back
to us the complex and loved personality and life of the
one we miss.

Conversely, one of the saddest mistakes survivors make
is, out of their pain, never to speak of the loved one again.
Such silence, far from diminishing the pain, just causes it
to build up and may result in life-pervading bitterness.

So let's talk. Let's remember. Of course, not every occasion with family and friends is an occasion for recalling.
But we are more apt to err on the side of silence.

I know that talking about a loved one is good medicine!

DECEMBER 20

When I say "I fear"—don't let it disturb you, dearest heart. We all fear when we are in waiting rooms. Yet we must pass beyond them . . . All this sounds very strenuous and serious. But now that I have wrestled with it, it's no longer so. I feel happy—deep down. All is well.

—KATHERINE MANSFIELD

Katherine Mansfield was writing to her husband. It was her own imminent death, and own fear, she was writing about.

We who mourn our loved ones are, in a sense, left in the waiting room, not knowing what it is like to pass beyond. But if we see that the one who is about to pass through has lost all fear, and has confidence, after a long struggle, that all is well—surely that diminishes our fear, too. And raises our hope for what lies on the other side of the door when we shall be summoned into the mystery.

After the struggle and the fear . . . comes peace.

I dreamed I fell through a trap door—into subterranean
terrors.

—HOYT HICKMAN

It will always be there—the occasion of loss, the memory
of its onset and pain, the diminishing but real possibility
that at any moment we could be plunged back into it.

There is a way in which we would not want this otherwise. To take away all the sharpness of our loss could
take away the intensity of our relationship with the loved
one.

At first, we are always falling through the trapdoor. This
image occurred to me again and again—as it did to my
husband—in those early years of dealing with the death
of our daughter.

But it is possible to climb back out, or to reestablish our
footing after the trapdoor drops. And in time, we will find
we have some choice about it—whether we will skirt that
close to emotional crisis or not. It is not always a bad
choice to do so. It is good news when we find we have a
choice at all.

◆◆

*Even through the experience of this pain, I am grateful for the
intensity of my love for the one I have lost.*

Every bone in my body aches individually with a dragging weariness of pain, and the joints cry aloud for a
warm balm; honeyed oil, to be poured, engulfing me,
into the rusty sockets. Soporifics, drugs, nectars, elixirs,
etc., I want them all; anything to transform me, to make
me different, to forget myself even for a second.
—CAITLIN THOMAS

Sound familiar? If we could just get out of our skin, be
someone else's awareness. If we could just forget about
this terrible loss for a little while.

But when we do forget—in sleep or some other diversion—the return is so painful that the temporary reprieve
is hardly worth it.

What are we to do?

Be careful. Careful not to do something destructive of
ourselves—like overindulge in alcohol or tranquilizers.
Careful of our general health and safety.

And then bear with the suffering, knowing that, incredible though it may seem now, it will ease.

Something my son once said comes to mind. It was not
long after his sister had died in an accident, and our whole
family was terribly distraught. In the midst of his grief,
and from some pool of wisdom to which he had access,
he calmly said, "It'll take time, but we'll feel good again."

It'll take time, but I'll feel good again.

. . . memory nourishes the heart, and grief abates.
—MARCEL PROUST

At this season of the year—so filled with memories and, for most people, family occasions—sometimes our grief seems all but unbearable. And grief *is* often especially sharp around holiday occasions.

But after a while we begin to savor the recall of those gathered times when we were all together, when the tenor of the days was festive and mutually cherishing. If our loved one had a particular role in the rituals of this season, we who take over that role may feel a special bond with the one who is gone.

So memory "nourishes the heart," eases the sharp edges of grief, and, whether or not we speak of it to one another, spreads its arms to comfort and to gather us as one family in the great human stream of life.

In my memory I can live with my loved one again, and be glad.

DECEMBER 24

Again at Christmas did we weave
   The holly round the Christmas hearth;
   The silent snow possess'd the earth,
And calmly fell our Christmas-eve.

The yule-log sparkled keen with frost,
   No wing of wind the region swept,
   But over all things brooding slept
The quiet sense of something lost.

—ALFRED TENNYSON

Holidays are among the hardest times for those who have lost a loved one. They are so fraught with family ritual, the layered memories of years.

Sometimes we feel free to talk about it—indeed, there's no way *not* to talk about it if the grief is fresh.

But after some time has passed, when the grief is in the background but not really yet assimilated into our lives, it may be even harder—the dull ache of absence, and everyone trying to be cheerful.

One year—the first year we tried to go back to our usual Christmas patterns—the unspoken gloom hovered behind our attempts at joy and repartee. Suddenly, almost as though by unspoken direction, we gathered in a circle, our arms around one another, and acknowledged our grief. Then we could get on with Christmas.

In this season I will find hope, and grief as well.

Where there is great love, there are always miracles.
—WILLA CATHER

Every religion has its miracles. For Christians, the miracle of Christ's life, death, and resurrection; for Jews, the escape from Egypt and manna in the wilderness; for Muslims, the ascension of Mohammed from Jerusalem to Heaven.

And we have our own miracles of love—our family stories of reconciliations, of recoveries that defy medical explanation but are laid to someone's faith. Perhaps in our faith communities we see other miracles of love—the dispossessed made to feel at home, the hungry fed, bonds of understanding and mutual joy forming across cultural and racial differences. And in our society at large we see, again and again, the outpouring of food and clothing and shelter to unknown victims of disaster.

Of course there are glitches—in personal relationships as in international efforts. Others are not always sensitive to our needs—nor are we to theirs. Given that each of us inhabits a unique and private world, maybe it's a miracle that we get along as well as we do. So at this season of celebration and longing, let's raise a glass or an inner hurrah, even in our sadness, for the gifts of love wherever we find them—in strangers, in our loved ones, and in our own hearts as well.

I will open my heart to the love that is around me.

DECEMBER 26

Time does restore to us our quiet joy in the spiritual presence of those we love, so that we learn to remember without pain, and to speak without choking up with tears. But all our lives we will be subject to sudden small reminders which will bring all the old loss back overwhelmingly.

—ELIZABETH WATSON

Particularly at this time of year when families are celebrating the holidays, the "sudden small reminders"—and the large ones, too—come to plague us. We thought we were doing so well, and then there we are, crying as though our loss was yesterday.

We need to take heart. If our loss is recent, the sadness is understandably overwhelming. If it was a while ago and we thought we were over the worst, then perhaps this time it will not take so long for "the quiet joy" to reassert itself, the spiritual presence to return in its quiet and infinitely precious way.

Our life runs in seasons, as does our grief. Some seasons are long, some short. But if we are resolute in our efforts to be present to the moment, even as we know this moment will give way to another, we can be assured at these times of renewed pain that things will get better.

◆◆

When I am feeling my most grief-stricken, may I hold in some place in my heart the promise that I will feel better.

Love is the heartbeat of all life.

> —PARAMAHANSA YOGANANDA

We feel it in ourselves—this mysterious generative force that enables us to reach out to the stranger in need, as well as to those on whom we depend to nourish and share our lives. Our need to love others is as constant as the beating of our hearts. So we build a network of life support and life enhancement, and much of the meaning of our lives plays itself out along that network.

Then one of the main components of the network is taken from us. It throws our lives for a loop. The whole system is in disarray.

But the energy is still there. Love is not a finite, limited quality, any more than the energy set loose in creation can be fully contained, sealed, or spent.

The love we lavished on the one who is gone continues to move toward that person. But in our sorrow love seems to extend itself, and in tenderhearted compassion we recognize how bound together we all are—life to life, fragment to fragment, love to love.

The love that bound me to the departed binds us all.

DECEMBER 28

"But, Gran, is everything really all right? Really?" It is completely cosmic questioning, coming from a small girl in a white nightgown with a toothbrush in her hand, sensing the unfamiliar surrounding the familiar . . . I must answer it for her, looking down at her serious, upturned face . . .

"Yes, Lena, it is all right."

And the two little girls and I climb into the fourposter bed to sing songs and tell stories.

—MADELEINE L'ENGLE

"Is everything really all right? Really?" Though it assumes different aspects at different times, it is our most basic question. It is behind our ventures into theology and ethics, behind our anguished dreams, our fears and hopes as we stand at the bedside of loved ones, as we confront the mystery of death.

There is no way we can know all the particulars on how "all right" everything is. But if we can trust that behind life's mysteries and dilemmas there is a Creator who knows what is going on and who wishes us well, that's a very good start.

And then what? What could be better than to sing songs and tell stories?

I will trust the life that surrounds and upholds me to see me through.

In a dark time, the eye begins to see.

—THEODORE ROETHKE

When one walks out into darkness, at first it is hard to see anything. Then the eyes adapt to this loss of light and, bit by bit, we begin to see—probably to see things we'd have passed over quickly had we walked by them in full light.

Something like that happens with suffering. Not that we would have chosen it. Not that we like it at all. But after a while, against our will, against our better judgment, we realize that we have acquired some wisdom through all this pain. Our sense of what is important is heightened. We're not so easily disturbed by petty things. We may make different uses of our time. Perhaps we reevaluate the demands we make of ourselves and drop some from the list. It was quite a revelation to me to realize in the wake of my daughter's death that I didn't have to take responsibility for the social ease of any situation in which I found myself. There are worse things than awkward silences.

We will probably find, among other things, that we are drawn to those who are experiencing fresh grief. We, more than most, can stand with them, so that in their dark time they will begin to see.

We who have dwelt in darkness begin to see.

DECEMBER 30

I know my children are concerned about me, but I am all right and I am glad they are letting me have a few days to myself now and then. Their mother taught them to care and I see her hand in all of this. I guess I should think of it as her staying around to watch over me.

—TERRY KAY

When a family member dies, the survivors are faced with the delicate task of caring for each other, filling in the space left vacant by the loved one.

Some things like filling out papers and attending to financial matters are self-evident. Others, like the degree of comfort and presence a bereaved person needs or wants, are difficult to judge, and it takes a while to get the balance right. It is important to recognize good intentions, and also to speak up, kindly, when the balance sways too far to one side or the other.

In this back and forth of who does best and most wisely for whom, the loved one's absence is keenly felt—otherwise, why would we be doing all this? But maybe the loved one's presence is here, too—in the care we take of each other, in the tenderness with which we try to fill the unfillable shoes.

I will try to be honest and kind in dealing with the responses of others to my loss.

It is dark now. The snow is deep blue and the ocean nearly black. It is time for some music.

—MAY SARTON

In the midst of the deepest winter, of the darkest night, what are we to do?

Acknowledge the cold and the dark, the mystery of an unknowable black ocean that seems to stretch into infinity . . . and then sing!

Or, to put it another way, "It is better to light a candle than to curse the darkness."

One of the glories of human beings is their ability to venture, to see beyond the immediate scene, to raise a note of hope and risk in a sometimes foreboding world.

So may this New Year's Eve—this turning into the next year, this milestone which has its aura of sadness because I enter another year without my loved one—may this New Year's Eve be for me a time for music. And if I am able— later, if not now—may I hear in my heart the voice of my loved one lifted with my voice, to praise life, to hope for life, to join others on this circling globe in an "Alleluia," for the experiences we have shared and share even now, and for the ways beyond time and death in which we are bound to one another in gratitude and love.

Happy New Year. Alleluia. Amen.